GOD
STRONG

GOD
STRONG

★ ★ ★ ★ ★

THE MILITARY WIFE'S
SPIRITUAL SURVIVAL GUIDE

SARA HORN

ZONDERVAN®

ZONDERVAN.com/
AUTHORTRACKER
follow your favorite authors

ZONDERVAN

God Strong
Copyright © 2010 by Sara Horn

This title is also available as a Zondervan ebook. Visit www.zondervan.com/ebooks.

This title is also available in a Zondervan audio edition. Visit www.zondervan.fm.

Requests for information should be addressed to:
Zondervan, *Grand Rapids, Michigan 49530*

Library of Congress Cataloging-in-Publication Data

Horn, Sara, 1977 –
    God strong : the military wife's spiritual survival guide / Sara Horn.
      p.   cm.
    Includes bibliographical references.
    ISBN 978-0-310-29402-3 (softcover)
      1. Wives — Religious life. 2. Christian women — Religious life. 3. Military spouses — Religious
life. I. Title.
    BV4528.15.H67   2010
    248.8'435088355 — dc22
                                              2009032593

Published in association with the literary agency of Alive Communications, Inc., 7680 Goddard
Street, Suite 200, Colorado Springs, CO 80920. www.alivecommunications.com

Interior design: Matthew Van Zomeren

Printed in the United States of America

09 10 11 12 13 14 15 16 17 • 23 22 21 20 19 18 17 16 15 14 13 12 11 10 9 8 7 6 5 4 3 2 1

To every military wife who has ever asked,
"How can I do this?"

CONTENTS

God said this once and for all;
how many times
Have I heard it repeated?
"Strength comes
Straight from God."
—Psalm 62:11

"But my people—oh, I'll make them strong, GOD-strong!
and they'll live my way." GOD says so!
—Zechariah 10:12

CHAPTER ONE

The Difference One Word Makes

★ ★ ★ ★ ★

IF STRENGTH IS SYMBOLIZED BY COLOR, the summer of 2007 I would have been invisible. That was the midway point of my husband's first deployment to Iraq, and a crumpled-up piece of paper in my wastebasket had more strength than I did at the time.

The Fourth of July had arrived and I was alone. All my friends had decided to go out of town that week, and so it was just my little boy and me, and I didn't want to do anything. While other families were out grilling in their back yards and enjoying the holiday, I was missing my husband, Cliff, and ruefully thinking about how our family's sacrifice was giving other families the chance to carry on with their carefree lives. I tried to put on a brave face for our son, but that day, it wasn't working very well. So I sent Caleb out to play in the bright sunshine with the neighbor kids while I sat on my couch with the curtains closed staring blankly at nothing in particular. I was done. I was worn out. I had nothing left to give. I tried to pray, but even that was hard.

Just a little over a year before, I sat in that exact same spot, thinking about the news Cliff had called with from his AT (annual training). His Navy Reserve Seabee battalion would deploy at the beginning of 2007.

At the time, I was very optimistic about and even motivated by the deployment. Cliff had been in the Navy Reserves for a little over ten years, but I had never really felt like a true military wife. I didn't buy our groceries at the commissary; Cliff didn't wear his camouflage to work every day. In fact, my husband's Reserve center was in Millington, near Memphis, almost four hours from where we lived in Nashville. I could count on one hand the number of times I'd visited the base with him on a drill weekend during his first decade of service. I'd never met Cliff's commanding officer, never attended any special ceremonies or worried about any military formalities.

For our family, military life was never really the norm. We got used to the one weekend a month, two weeks a year that Cliff was "gone to Navy," as our little boy called it, and we liked the little bit of extra paycheck that came with it, but for the most part, Cliff's service as a reservist was never really part of our family's day-to-day. Until it interfered with a birthday or an anniversary or some other special event; in those cases, we definitely had something in common with active military.

Only when I traveled twice to Iraq in 2003 to cover stories of Christians in the military did I finally get a glimpse of what it means to be in the military, what it means for the families and spouses back home. I interviewed both service members and their families and wrote stories about how families can stay connected, how God can give hope in stressful times, and how service members can keep their faith strong. I shared with my readers the ups and downs of deployment and the difficult challenges faced by military wives when they had to watch their husbands leave to fight a war. I admired the wives' quiet strength, their resilience, and their commitment to their husbands and their families through extremely tough circumstances. When we got word about our own deployment, I wondered if I could be like those wives I'd gotten to know. At the time, it felt like I was about to play dress-up, wearing a costume that wasn't made for me.

But now, fifteen months later, I definitely felt like a military wife. I knew what it was like to carry my cell phone with me everywhere, including to bed; I watched the news and wondered if my husband was in the area where they were reporting violence; I knew the pain of sitting by myself at church and feeling completely alone in a room filled with people; I sometimes cried when I saw a soldier in uniform; I knew what it was like to force myself to answer with a pleasant "I'm good" when someone asked me how I was doing, knowing they didn't want to hear how I really felt.

But sitting on the couch that day, worn out, spent, and ready to quit with no clear idea how I could do that, I came to another realization: that the strength I'd run on for so long was only my own and that already seven months into the deployment, I was missing what God was trying to teach me. That *my* strength had absolutely nothing to do with it.

This was a hard truth to swallow. I'd read everything I could get my hands on about the proverbial job description of a military spouse, and of all the requirements that people talked about, strength was the biggest. Strength was the most important. If you didn't have it, you wouldn't survive. You had to be strong for your husband. You had to be strong for your kids. You had to be strong when you least expected it: when well-meaning friends made comments that made you want to wilt; when strangers told you exactly what they thought about the war your husband was fighting; when you saw couples out walking hand in hand. You had to be strong when the car broke down and your child got sick and the garage door wouldn't open and the dog threw up on your already not-so-clean carpet. You had to be strong for yourself, because there was no one else who would be.

I had thrown my military wife dress-up clothes on with such focus and determination that I hadn't put on the most important garment. My faith. Instead of wearing my faith in God as my favorite piece and depending on it each day, I had treated it like an accessory I sometimes picked up and often put down, counting on my own confidence, my own determination, and my own stick-to-itiveness to get me through. I was making it, but sometimes barely. I was determined, but there were major struggles. I was strong, but my strength was coming from one very weak source. Me.

Two Common Misperceptions

As military wives, we pride ourselves on making do. Hanging tough. Keeping it together. And when things don't go so well? We just bear down harder, work longer, and *make* it happen, right?

When you find yourself in a difficult situation or challenge — maybe your husband is out of town and you're dealing with sick kids and broken-down appliances, or you're struggling together over money and financial pressures — whatever finds you at the end of your rope, more than once you may hear yourself repeating, "God won't give me more than I can handle. God won't give me more than I can handle."

"God won't give me more than I can bear or handle." Most of us are familiar with this saying, and we usually repeat it when we're right in the thick of it. We're talking with a friend about all of our troubles and then we shrug our shoulders and say it. As if that magic phrase will suddenly wipe away all of the difficulty; as if, obviously, we should be able to handle it, because if God says he won't give us more than we can bear, then we should have no problem handling everything that gets thrown at us. Right?

What would you say if I told you that God never actually said that? That this saying isn't even in the Bible?

Misperception 1: God doesn't give me more than I can bear, so it's up to me to handle it. The verse of Scripture that this saying gets its basis from is 1 Corinthians 10:13. Take a look: "No test or temptation that comes your way is beyond the course of what others have had to face. All you need to remember is that God will never let you down; he'll never let you be pushed past your limit; he'll always be there to help you come through it."

Notice that this verse is referring to *temptation*. The New Living Translation puts it this way: "But remember that the temptations that come into your life are no different from what others experience. And God is faithful. He will keep the temptation from becoming so strong that you can't stand up against it. When you are tempted, he will show you a way out so that you will not give in to it."

This verse is talking about what happens when you're faced with another lonely night because your husband is away or working late and you are tempted to get online and strike up a conversation with a stranger. Or call up an old boyfriend you still occasionally talk to. Or at midnight, eat more of the double-chocolate cheesecake you had at dinner. Maybe all of it. Now *that's* temptation! This Scripture verse says God will never allow us to face temptations that we can't stand against, that we can't walk away from.

Notice, though, it never says God won't let you experience great stress in your life or deal with a great challenge or even keep you from being pushed to what feels like your breaking point.

When we buy into this misperception that God won't give us more than we can handle, we buy into the idea that it's up to *us* to make it work. And when it doesn't work, and we're exhausted and worn out, we blame ourselves, because obviously we're doing something wrong. And this is where we're missing it; it has very little to do with us.

Psalm 121:1 tells us "[our] strength comes from GOD." Psalm 62:11 says it as well: "Strength comes straight from God." God tells Paul in 2 Corinthians 12:9 that his strength "works best" in Paul's weakness (NLT).

Do you see it? Do you get it? That it's not *our* strength that matters? We're not talking about our muscles or our sheer will or determination. We're talking about spiritual muscle. God's muscle. *God does the most when we can do only the very least.*

I was reminded of this important lesson the other day when I was sitting in the car line at my son's school. Yes, I confess. I'm one of *those* moms who will get to the school an hour before classes actually end so I can be at the front of the line and leave first and avoid the tedious process of getting through the line and cars stopping and going. But I also love that hour of quiet because I can read or write on my laptop or even pray if I want with no real distractions to interrupt me.

I was sitting there in the car line this particular afternoon and a kindergarten class was outside flying kites, enjoying the beautiful weather. The sun was out, warming the air just right, and the skies were blue with just a few puffy white clouds floating around. The kids were taking turns flying the kites. I noticed one little boy who had bright yellow curls and one very red face. Each time it was his turn to fly the kite, he would grab the end of the string, get the kite up in the air, and run as fast as his little legs could take him. Around and around the yard he went, the kite flying blissfully up in the air behind him.

But I noticed something unusual. Not once did the little boy ever look back at the kite. Not once did he ever stop to let the wind take off with it and just watch it go. So intent was he on doing all the work to keep that kite up that he was missing the joy of seeing it in the air at all.

Just as that little boy will one day learn to trust the wind to keep his kite up in the air, we too must learn to trust in God's strength in all of our circumstances. But it's not always an easy task.

Why is it so hard for us to take our hands off the steering wheel and let God drive? Why is it so hard for us to fathom the idea of not even sitting in the passenger seat or pushing behind the car but actually putting ourselves in the trunk? Now *that* is fully relying on God's strength!

I think it has a lot to do with the second misperception that we have grown up to believe.

Misperception 2: God helps those who help themselves, so I should do as much of it as I can. This is another one of those sayings that we've quoted so much we think it's true, and we say it just as freely as we quote John 3:16. The difference, though, is that "God helps those who help themselves" can't be found in the Bible. This is actually a quote from Benjamin Franklin that first appeared in *Poor Richard's Almanac* in 1757.

The Bible teaches the opposite. That God helps the helpless. He delights in being our strength. Matthew 9:36 tells us that when Jesus was among the people, his heart broke for them. "So confused and aimless they were, like sheep with no shepherd." They were helpless, as we are. But God wanted a relationship with us. Look what Paul tells us in Romans 5:6–8: "Christ arrives right on time to make this happen. He didn't, and doesn't, wait for us to get ready. He presented himself for this sacrificial death when we were far too weak and rebellious to do anything to get ourselves ready. And even if we hadn't been so weak, we wouldn't have known what to do anyway. We can understand someone dying for a person worth dying for, and we can understand how someone good and noble could inspire us to selfless sacrifice. But God put his love on the line for us by offering his Son in sacrificial death while we were of no use whatever to him."

"We were of no use whatever to him." Can you picture how that looks? We were of no use — weak and helpless, unable to help ourselves, certainly unable to help God.

And yet, as helpless and hopeless as we were, God still loved us enough to put his Son on the cross for us. Because as much as we resist asking for help — from others and from God — he wants to love us and be the strength and support we need.

I know a military wife whose husband is currently deployed for a year to eighteen months, and she is home with their six children, the youngest born just a month ago and the oldest just fourteen. Even though she was on bed rest for the majority of her pregnancy, I don't believe she ever asked anyone for help. And when I recently called her with an offer from a church community group that wanted to help her do some things around her house, despite sounding exhausted and worn out, she was still extremely reluctant to accept the help. And there are many of us just like her. But God wants to help the helpless! Sometimes that's in the form of sending others to share our problems and our struggles. We must come to a point where we can accept that depending only on our strength just doesn't work.[1]

THE REAL SOURCE OF OUR STRENGTH

I know that by now you may be squirming. Me too! This idea of accepting that we're helpless doesn't make us feel so good. We certainly don't feel strong. And isn't that what this book is supposed to be about? Being strong? Yes. And no. Let me explain.

Strength is one of the recruitment themes the Army has used in recent years. "There's strong. And then there's Army

Strong." You've probably heard it. The idea is that there are different strengths represented within the Army branch of the service, and when you're a part of the Army, you are much stronger for it. This theme reinforces the notion that the whole is greater than the sum of its parts. As an individual, you are stronger as a part of the group than you are by yourself. Your strength is reinforced by the strengths of others, so you're no longer just strong, you're Army Strong.

Wives have given this theme a bit of a twist. There's "Army Wife Strong" or "Military Wife Strong." A "hooah" for the strength, determination, and just plain grit of the military spouse. Of course, there's also the phrase that could have been created only by a military wife: "Put on your Big Girl Panties," the more feminine version of pulling yourself up by the bootstraps. I first heard this when I spent a lot of time on military-spouse internet message boards. Many women use it as a reminder to themselves to be strong. To not give up. To roll with the punches, jump off the emotional roller coaster we find ourselves on, and just keep going.

The only problem is that Big Girl Panties can sometimes get lost. And often there may be no other military wives around to be Military Wife Strong and stand in solidarity with. You may really and truly be all by yourself. And then what happens to your strength? Your determination? Your hope?

When I buy into the misperceptions we've already talked about—that God won't give me more than I can handle, so I must handle it, and that God helps me when I help myself, so I better do it all—I become so focused on my own willpower, my own resolve, and my own tenacity that I start running on borrowed time. Eventually that man-made fuel burns up. Eventually you find yourself sitting on the couch with the curtains drawn, wondering how you can face another day. And though, just like a car, I can probably refuel, that energy source can be expensive and take a while to fill up.

There is a better way.

There is a better source.

There is Someone we're forgetting.

When we no longer rely on strength from within but instead rely on strength from above, it is no longer up to us to be the strong ones. Because it's no longer *about* us.

When we replace our strength with God's strength, we discover a major difference. The burdens and the problems and the heartaches we carry around with our own strength don't disappear, but they do feel a little lighter. We don't have to push and pull and lug and grunt our way through. Instead, we can walk with God and rely on his muscle to do the heavy lifting. It's like carrying a heavy large box up a flight of stairs. To do it by yourself is not just hard but exhausting. If you lift it with someone else who has the muscle power to carry most of the weight, it's better. It's easier. It's doable. We see a major difference, not just in actually moving the box but in our perspective.

Isaiah tells us that God "gives strength to the weary and increases the power of the weak" (Isaiah 40:29 NIV). He reminds us that when we put our hope in God, our strength is renewed. We can ride on the backs of eagles. We can run and not get tired. We can walk and not grow faint. We can become God Strong.

None of this can happen, though, when we try to do it ourselves.

BECOMING GOD STRONG

Since starting Wives of Faith, a faith-based support organization for military wives, I've had the privilege and blessing to meet a lot of military wives—active, reserve, National Guard, retired, and even several individual ready reserve (IRR). These women come in all sorts of shapes and sizes and have different personalities, backgrounds, views, and hopes and dreams for themselves and their families. Some love the military. Some hate it. Some put up with it. Some have a strong faith in God. Some are just feeling their way toward a relationship with him. There are a lot of differences. But there are also a lot of similarities. They share the same fears and worries, many of the same struggles and challenges, the same questions and concerns. And they love their husbands.

Whether you're a new Christian or a longtime spiritual warrior, there are nine spiritual truths that as military wives we need to know to be God Strong—nine truths I will be covering in the next nine chapters. Some of these truths address the negative aspects we bring into our lives, like fear and loneliness, worry, and the all-consuming idea of being superwomen. Other truths address the promises God gives us when it comes to joy and trust, hope and love. We will talk a little bit about our marriages and our children, but mostly we will focus on being the women God wants us to be, embracing the call he has given to each of us in our own specific seasons as military wives and learning all that he wants to teach us.

One of the benefits of connecting with other military wives through online message boards or groups like Wives

Survival Sisters
Little Purple Wildflowers

It has been a tough week. We're in the middle of my husband's deployment, and I've been feeling like I've reached a breaking point. It's hard to think I can keep going through this deployment, being separated from my love.

I'm a very young, newly married Army wife without children While most of the time I view this as a blessing, not having to care for little ones without the help of my spouse, there are other times I am greatly aware of being completely alone. This week is one of those times, and depression has set in. I've slept in until ten, stayed in my pajamas, and watched movies, eaten ice cream, and cried a lot.

My husband really worries about me when I get like this, because really there's nothing he can do to help. He's always pushing and encouraging me to get out of the house, get sunshine, and do fun stuff while he's gone. To my shame, there are many times I resist and fight this encouragement. First of all, I'm just not a very energetic, outdoorsy kind of person. I also get frustrated because I feel a lot of guilt in enjoying myself without him, and sometimes doing fun stuff makes me less accessible to talk to him, which makes me feel horrible. But still, he encourages, and yesterday, I finally listened.

I took an adventure. I packed a bag with my Bible, camera, and a few books, and took off, my windows down, sunroof open, and radio off. I went back to a little country road I had discovered a few weeks ago quite by accident, and I drove until it dead-ended. As I was turning around in someone's driveway, right before me was an amazing view of the Texas hill country, so I decided to get out of the car to take a few pictures and capture the beauty.

On my way back, I noticed a deer in someone's front yard. Again, I snapped a few pictures. I was about to drive off when another deer came out of the clearing. I was so glad I took some time and didn't drive off so quickly! Continuing on my way, I turned right onto another country road I knew would take me out to Stillhouse Hollow Lake, a park area my husband and I had visited about a year ago.

The first thing I noticed was all the little purple wildflowers. I had to smile because just a few weeks ago Russ had told me he wanted me to "go somewhere where there are flowers," because he thought they would make me feel better. Well, they certainly did!

I love Stillhouse Hollow Lake because it is a man-made reservoir, so the water is extremely blue and very peaceful. I was reminded of the verse in Psalm 46 that says, "Be still and know that I am God" (v. 10). I sat there for a few minutes just basking in the sunlight and warmth of the day. It was nice to be able to sit and think, to pray, and to meditate on God's love. I then pulled out my Bible and God directed me to some of my favorite passages of Scripture in Isaiah 40 and 41. Take a moment to read those chapters if you're not familiar with them.

Sometimes it is easy for me to feel like God can't really see and know what is going on in my life, like my way is "hidden from the Lord" (Isaiah 40:27). Sometimes it's easy to feel like I honestly don't have enough strength to get through another day alone without losing my last shred of sanity. But I know if I keep waiting on the Lord, I will be okay.

It's hard not to struggle sometimes to be "Army Strong!" and get through it all, but I don't think that's what God wants from me. He says to me, "Aprille, it's okay to be weak today. Because when you are weak, I will be strong for you. Just wait on me and stop trying to hold yourself together. Let me help you. Let me be with you. Let me love you."

I am not alone, even when it feels like I am. God is with me, and he will help me get through this.

As I drove back home, I felt encouraged, happy, loved, and incredibly thankful for my husband. Sometimes I get frustrated by the differences between Russ and me, but God is perfect in wisdom and I find myself learning from Russ. Learning to try new things, to move out of my comfort zone and do things I normally wouldn't do. I'm a homebody and would love to just stay at home and watch movies all day, but think of just how much I would have missed yesterday! I would have missed a time of closeness with the only one who can give me strength for this deployment. I would have missed enjoying his creation. I would have missed his love.

— *Aprille Donaldson,*
Army wife

of Faith is sharing our stories with one another. When I hear from another wife about her experience, I realize I'm not so alone, and I'm reminded that if God can work in her life, he can work in mine too.

For this reason, I wanted to include stories from other wives, which you'll find in the "Survival Sisters" sections of each chapter. Consider these wives to be like the friends you go for walks with or meet at the gym to work out with. You'll also find "Strength Builders" and "Strength Trainers" for your personal use, as well as to use with a group, if you choose to read this book with others. My prayer is that these tools will help keep your focus where it needs to be: on God and his Word.

Look at what Jesus said when he was talking to the crowds one day: "Are you tired? Worn out? Burned out on religion? Come to me. Get away with me and you'll recover your life. I'll show you how to take a real rest. Walk with me and work with me — watch how I do it. Learn the unforced rhythms of grace. I won't lay anything heavy or ill-fitting on you. Keep company with me and you'll learn to live freely and lightly" (Matthew 11:28 – 30).

Receiving and relying on God's strength cannot happen overnight. We've been conditioned to do everything ourselves our entire lives, so it's impossible to simply flick a switch and turn over everything for God to handle right away. But as we spend more time in prayer and Bible study and develop and apply the spiritual truths we're going to be talking about, we will be able to lean more on his strength and less on our own. That's my prayer for all of us. Get ready for an exciting journey as we discover what it means to be God Strong.

STRENGTH BUILDERS

"God is good, a hiding place in tough times. He recognizes and welcomes anyone looking for help, no matter how desperate the trouble" (Nahum 1:7).

"Be strong. Take courage. Don't be intimidated. Don't give them a second thought because GOD, your God, is striding ahead of you. He's right there with you. He won't let you down; he won't leave you" (Deuteronomy 31:6).

"God-devotion makes a country strong; God-avoidance leaves people weak" (Proverbs 14:34).

STRENGTH TRAINERS

1. What does it mean to be God Strong? If you could visualize a person who is God Strong, what does she look like?

2. On a scale of 1 to 10, with 10 being the easiest, how easy is it for you to rely on God's strength and not your own? If your answer is low, what can you do to change it?

3. Name one area of your life where you know you will struggle in leaning on God's strength and not just on your own. Ask God to help you overcome this.

4. As a military wife, how hard is it to handle everything on your own? How would it feel to lean on God more? What would the difference be?

CHAPTER TWO

MY STRENGTH COMES FROM GOD

★ ★ ★ ★ ★

ONE OF THE HARDEST PARTS of the military life is the deployment. Being separated from your spouse can be emotionally grueling, depressingly solitary, and overwhelming. If you let it be that way.

During our first deployment, I was determined that it would *not* be that way. I approached this new experience in our lives with the fervor and determination of the defenders of the Alamo; whatever happened, I would not let our family down. I had a plan. I would be the Great Communicator, keeping my husband and son and the rest of our family and friends closely connected; I would be the Great Organizer, juggling all of my son's activities, my work responsibilities, church functions, and aforementioned family communications with the ease and skill of one who knows no scheduling conflict. I would be the Great Cheerleader, offering an unending supply of encouragement to my husband in Iraq and to our son here at home. And to do all of this, I would have to be the Great Health Nut. Yes, that was my plan. I would eat right, exercise every day, and stay fit and healthy, stress free, and positively motivated throughout the deployment. I would be physically, mentally, and emotionally strong. Those incredible endorphins would keep me going!

To help in this quest for überstrength (or what I ultimately learned is Me Strength), I brought along my iPod to the gym, loaded with the music I thought I needed to "get in the zone." There were songs on there I had never listened to before but had bought specifically for the deployment—titles like "Fighter" and "Push It" and "Let's Get It Started." I chose songs that encouraged me to push myself, to make my life happen how I wanted it to happen, to be sexy (after all, I wanted to look good when my husband came home!), to be a rock star or at least to live the confident rock star life. The other songs I owned—songs praising God, songs that reminded me of his goodness, his grace, and his control—were left off my playlist because I'd decided they weren't intense enough. Not motivating enough. I needed fast and loud. I needed tough and strong.

What I didn't realize until months later, when I was so spent and worn out and sitting on my couch in the dark, was that I had overlooked God's strength. I had fooled myself into thinking that because I was Me Strong, I didn't have to be God Strong. God was there, but at a distance safe enough to keep me from being reminded just how weak I am.

Me Strength versus God Strength

Developing strong muscles doesn't happen instantly. Neither does growing spiritual ones. But relying on God's strength and learning how to embrace him and his values and teachings are daily lessons we can't miss. His instruction is free and available to us; it is our availability to him that often goes missing.

In the military life, strength is everything, and that mindset is brought home to us by our husbands. Strength of body. Strength of mind. We need strength of courage. We must develop and maintain strength with honor and duty and doing what's right. But weakness is never welcome. Weakness is a weed that threatens bodies and spirits; whether physically or emotionally, being weak can hurt not just one but many. Weakness can hurt a platoon just as it can hurt a marriage. A squad can be damaged; a family crippled.

Because we fear being weak so much, we go out of our way to be strong. But as I mentioned in the last chapter, we can go only so far on our own strength, and when we can't move another muscle, we automatically think there's something wrong. I'm not doing something right. My faith must not be where it should be.

But our weaknesses are not reflections of our faith; our weaknesses are just reflections of our humanity.

We're human. We mess up, we make mistakes, and regardless of what branch of the military we're in and whether we embrace our military-wife titles with enthusiasm or cynicism, our supplies of strength often come up short. Things don't go as planned. Life throws curveballs we can't hit. We grow tired. We fail. We're unable to do what we need to do, and when that happens, we hang our heads and beat ourselves up and moan and groan and wonder why we can't handle being military wives any better than we can handle life. We duck our heads when friends say, "You're so strong," because really, we know different. And we wonder where God is and why we can't do better.

Paul knew about weakness. His "thorn in the flesh" stayed with him and tormented him throughout his life. He struggled with this flaw constantly. Though we don't know exactly what it was (perhaps a disease or a chronic illness), it was troublesome enough that Paul begged God to take it from him three different times (2 Corinthians 12:7–8).

Have you ever made a similar request of God? Lord, just take this problem away. God, if you would only make me stronger. Jesus, if you would only let this happen, then this would turn out the way I want it to. But as Paul knew, we often discover that it is only through our weaknesses that God makes us stronger. As God told Paul, "My grace is enough; it's all you need. My strength comes into its own in your weakness" (2 Corinthians 12:9). And how did Paul respond? He let Christ take over. And his faith was strengthened through his weakness.

When you have moments of feeling like you have no strength left, it isn't necessarily an indication you have no faith left. When you wonder whether you can continue on in a marriage in which your spouse is around only half the time, you must remind yourself that God can be relied on to meet all of your needs (Philippians 4:19). When you are struggling with feeling inadequate for the tasks you face each day, you can rely on the knowledge that God is faithful (1 Corinthians 1:9), that he's consistent and trustworthy, and that he will help you (Isaiah 50:7). When overwhelmed by negative emotions, you can hold on to God's promise that he is with you and that he will quiet you with his love (Zephaniah 3:17).

Feelings can't be indicators of your faith or belief, because feelings come and go just as surely as sunshine and rain; belief and conviction are much more certain. The sun will come up every day regardless of whether I can see it. In *Mere Christianity*, C. S. Lewis writes that faith "is the art of holding on to things your reason has once accepted, in spite of your changing moods." We are emotional creatures, and whether we're going through deployments or other struggles in life, our emotions can often get the best of us. They are unreliable because they can change with the weather, by the month, the week, even the day.

Faith, however, is much more certain. Whatever the crazy inconsistent emotions I may feel right now, I can have faith that God will give me strength because he has done so before and because I have heard the stories of others whom he has strengthened, both in his Word and in the present day. I can hold tight to what Philippians 4:13 says: "Whatever I have, wherever I am, I can make it through anything in the One who makes me who I am."

I'll admit this is easier to say than to do, and it doesn't happen without some focus and concentration. Lewis even acknowledges that "the habit of Faith" must be trained;[2] we must practice what we believe. We must daily remind ourselves of what we accept as truth, or else we will forget and drift away.

Pretend you are in a kayak on the ocean. If you neglect to paddle, you'll still move, but at the whims of the wind and the current. Your boat is still in the water, but your focus has been on the shore, or maybe on the dark skies overhead. When you do pick up the paddle again, your movements will be a bit rustier, your paddling less smooth. Some time may pass until you once again find your rhythm. But if you keep paddling, regardless of what you see ahead, you will be better equipped to deal with high winds or rough waves when you encounter them. Your muscles will remember, stroke for stroke, what to do.

The same is true of faith. Keeping our faith in an active state rather than a dormant one—or worse, a catatonic one—through the good times, the easy times, keeps us ready for when we experience the harder moments life brings us. Weaknesses will always be there. But it is a different experience entirely when you realize that God's strength is carrying you through.

CRYING IN CHURCH

I don't know if you've ever experienced this, but when I was dealing with our deployment, church was often the last place I wanted to be. Oh, I went, because I wanted our son to go and have his normal routine, and I wanted to be able to update our Sunday school class and friends on how my husband was doing, but deep down inside, I didn't want to be there. I hated sitting by myself, because even in a room full of people like those in our class who we thought were like our second family, I was still by myself. I found it was like being in Noah's ark for an hour each week, watching couple after couple coming in two by two and then there was me, the lonely spouseless dove. (Though judging from how often others actually talked to me, maybe I was the skunk!)

The church service on Sunday mornings was just a little better because at least in there I was just one in a mass of bodies, and everyone's attention was directed toward the front instead of at each other. But this too presented a problem, because during the time of worship when we sang and prayed, my attention was forced, whether I liked it or not, straight on to the One whom I so often tried to avoid during the week. And that's when the tears would come.

I didn't enjoy the tears. To me, they might as well have rolled down my cheeks in bright neon orange shouting, "This military wife can't cut it!" I didn't like the looks of pity I tried to ignore and, worse, of those who pretended not to see.

What those tears should have reminded me, though, was that I could not be—I was not—strong enough on my own, but God was. He was the one I could turn to when I felt weak, because his strength is sustaining and accessible and available.

But I didn't like the tears and I didn't like feeling weak, so I kept God at arm's length much of the time. Yet I continued to struggle as I tried to be Me Strong, and I still cried in church on Sundays.

The strength we see in ourselves is usually a reflection of either how much we're allowing God in or how much we're allowing ourselves to get in the way. What do you see when you look for the sun to shine through a dirty pane of glass? We may catch a ray or two, but we won't see the light that was intended to glow brightly. We won't feel the warmth we could. When we put ourselves in the way, we miss experiencing God's full strength. We muddy up the glass with all of our own efforts and our own attempts, and we prevent ourselves from knowing what it feels like to be held, to be guided when we're lost, and to be supported when we're tired. To be lifted up when all we can do is limp.

Me Strength is messy. Undisciplined and unfocused. Me Strength runs hot and cold, in spurts and flashes, with no warning when it might give out. Me Strength tricks us into thinking something is easier when really, we're simply enduring. Me Strength requires work, backbreaking work. You will struggle with Me Strength. Sure, eventually you may accomplish what you set out to do, but it will be hard to get there.

God Strength, on the other hand, is steady. Fluid, constant, and consistent. There is quiet rest and tranquil knowledge with God Strength. There's an internal assurance you are not alone. When you feel God Strong, you feel the same security that a child feels being carried in a pair of strong arms and the joy a runner experiences when running ahead of the pack. With God Strength, there is no longer an inward focus but an upward view. Our hands aren't clenched along with our jaws in fierce determination. Instead, they're released and held out, a sign of our readiness to feel God's strength. To become God Strong.

I've experienced what it's like to go with Me Strength. But I've also seen what it means to be God Strong. As I write this, my husband has been without a full-time job for almost a year. His position at a nonprofit was eliminated six months after he came home from Iraq because of budget cuts, and it has been a struggle to find another job. Thankfully, he has his Navy drill weekends, but we still have experienced many of the very emotions I went through during our last deployment. Fear. The uncertainty of the unknown. Disappointment and frustration. All of these are familiar feelings. But something has been different this time. We have kept our focus on God. We are each praying more and we're praying together. I'm making more time to read the Bible and to study it. And there is a peace in our hearts that wasn't necessarily there during the deployment.

Let's be clear that I'm certainly not saying life is perfect. There are definitely days that are worse than others, when Me Strength tries to sneak back in. (Remember, our feelings

Survival Sisters
Changing My Focus

My fiancé, Jimmy, is active duty Army, a 1LT Mortar Platoon Leader, and at the time of this writing, he is deployed to Iraq. While we were still "just dating," I met with a close friend I consider my spiritual mentor as I was going back and forth over whether Jimmy and I should get married. Whether he, in fact, was "the one." At the time, I was really wrestling with everything that I *thought* was wrong with him. That's a whole other story, but she told me something so profound in the few times I met with her. She said, "You have to show him respect. You have to put him first."

Her advice came months before his deployment, when I was struggling over a lot of things in our relationship. I trust my friend with my life, so I gave it a shot. And she was so right when she told me that I would be surprised by the results. When I took the focus off myself and started doing nothing but serving him and showing him the utmost respect, the whole climate of our relationship changed. At the time, I was in Virginia and he was in Texas at Fort Hood, so we were dealing with all the common long-distance woes. He was stressed about the deployment, so he would explode at me when I complained that I wasn't getting enough attention. I was whiny and selfish and wanted as much of him as possible since I knew he would be leaving soon. I'm sorry to say most of our conversations were filled with choice words, hang-ups, and tears.

It's crazy what a little thing was at the core of our problems. I wrote him a letter in which I listed all the reasons I respect him. (I had read *Love and Respect* by Emerson Eggerichs, and this was a suggestion in the book.) I started biting my tongue when I was having a pity party and started putting Jimmy's needs before mine. When I finally was able to get to Texas for the few weeks before he left, I was amazed at the difference in myself and in our relationship. It was my goal to do everything I could for him as he moved out of his apartment, packed up his gear, and ran around town tying up loose ends. I set out to serve him, to respect him, and to meet his every need.

Within weeks after he left, he was begging me to marry him in emails and over Skype. Apparently my friend was right! Not only had we moved to the next stage of our relationship, but all of a sudden I realized all my needs were being met too. And even now—seven months into his being gone—he still meets my needs. I have a rough time, and he's there for me. I send him as many encouraging words as I can think of and a package a week—to meet his needs—and amazingly he has met all of mine. Not only are we happier, but I never think about my needs or the things I want from him. Because I keep my focus on him, I worry less about me, and somehow I am never in want. The greatest thing, though, is that I actually do have so much respect for him now. I constantly brag about him and realize what a blessing he is in my life. All because of a little respect.

It's the same thing Christ calls us to—to keep our eyes on him and keep our lives in his service. In Hebrews 12:1–3, the Lord tells us to keep our eyes fixed on Jesus, because from him will come the strength to persevere and shrug off what hinders us. Strength came when I was engaged in genuine service. It wasn't from my own doing. There was nothing I could have done to produce that change in our hearts. The strength in our relationship came from doing what we are called to, and it came from the Lord. It was so true in my relationship, and it's so true in life. We've got to put on the blinders and keep our focus pure. The blessings will come without our ever having to look for them.

— *Jennifer Showker,*
Army fiancée

are fickle, but our faith doesn't have to be.) There are still moments we wonder what God is up to; we wonder when this time of testing or growing or whatever he is doing in our lives will end or at least take a new direction. But there are more times than not when we feel a quiet confidence that God is in control. That he knows the way. And that he is carrying us, through the good and the bad. And that is what it means to be God Strong.

Just as Aaron and Joshua held up the arms of their friend Moses when he was too weak to keep going, so too does God support us. And when we're God Strong, we stop flailing and running in circles so much, and we start walking with a steadier gait. We stop feeling so weak, and we start feeling buoyed. We no longer try to do what was never intended — live on our own. Instead, we live with God leading, just a half step in front of us, allowing us to lean on him and encouraging us to follow all the way.

Buying into the Big Lie

As I was trying so hard to fit the image I had of what a military wife is supposed to be, I was buying into one of the oldest untruths around. That I really didn't need God; I was just fine on my own.

The Israelites were notorious for doing this. Throughout the Old Testament we find examples of this group, God's chosen people, displaying a very familiar pattern: people wander; people stray from God, relying on Me Strength instead of God Strength; people get into trouble, God intervenes; people repent and rededicate themselves to God. Little time passes, however, before it all starts over once again.

Look what God has to say about this in Jeremiah: "But my people have left me to worship the Big Lie. They've gotten off the track, the old, well-worn trail, and now bushwhack through underbrush in a tangle of roots and vines" (Jeremiah 18:15). In the New International Version of the Bible, God, speaking through Jeremiah, says, "My people have forgotten me."

How often we forget God until we have absolutely nowhere else to go. As military wives, we too struggle with the Big Lie. See if any of these statements sound familiar to you:

"I can take care of myself."

"I can do this."

"I'm the only one who knows what's best for me and my family."

"I don't need anyone's help."

"I'm the only one who can make this happen."

"If I don't do it, it doesn't get done."

"God's there if I need him, but I think I'm handling it pretty well."

When we accept the Big Lie that we can do life on our own power, we give up on God's Big Truth that "strength comes straight from God" (Psalm 62:11).

Go back to that verse in Jeremiah. "They've gotten off the track, the old, well-worn trail." God has already forged our way; just pick up the Bible and look through the pages and pages of other people's stories and challenges and perseverance. When they followed God's leading, they stayed on the trail already traveled. When they went their own way, they almost always found themselves at an impasse, unsure of what to do next. Notice that the trail isn't the one most comfortable or most familiar. It is a trail, however, that many have used before. And like those people before us, our only responsibility is to follow God's leading. He is already doing the heavy lifting, so why go in a different direction, dragging our burdens and our problems through an unclear, unmarked way? We already have the compass (God's Word); we already have the Heavy Lifter, whom we can lean on through prayer and daily interaction. What's missing? Our surrender.

Am I Not Sending You?

Gideon learned what surrender means when God gave him a special task. Once again, the Israelites had strayed from God and were experiencing all sorts of problems at the hands of the Midianites. Judges 6 tells us that an angel of the Lord appeared, sitting down under a tree near where Gideon was threshing wheat in a winepress.

"God is with you, O mighty warrior!" the angel said to Gideon.

Gideon must have stifled a laugh. Normally, wheat was threshed (the process of separating grain from the wheat's outer shell) out in big open fields, but because of the constant threat from the Midianites to raid the Israelites' land, Gideon was down in the pit of a winepress so he could thresh his wheat in peace and in safety. Here he was, a simple farmer who was hiding from the bad guys, and he was being called a warrior?

Gideon challenged God's messenger. After all, if God was really with him, why so many difficulties? Why turn them over to their enemies? "But now the LORD has abandoned us and put us into the hand of Midian" (Judges 6:13 NIV).

How often do we ask the same questions of God? "Why is this happening? I've tried to follow you and live a good life, so why am I still having problems? Why am I being forced to go through this? Where are you when I need you?"

But notice what God says to Gideon in verse 14. He doesn't acknowledge his complaints; he doesn't point out how the Israelites wound up in this mess in the first place; he simply tells Gideon to "go in the strength you have and save Israel out of Midian's hand" (NIV).

And then God adds one very important question. "Am I not sending you?"

Is God not sending you? Hasn't he placed you where you are today? As a wife, maybe as a mom, as a ministry leader or a business owner, and yes, as a military spouse; ask yourself, Would God send you and not enable you at the same time? No!

All of us are given special tasks and special purposes in life; some of us may have several over the course of our lifetime; in some cases, we may have just one or two. But you can be assured that God gives you the strength to go with it. He equips you for what he's asked you to do, whether it's raising a family, or running a business or a ministry; whether it's saying goodbye to your husband, whom you won't see for more than a year, or saying goodbye to friends you just made as you leave for a new duty station and a new town. He gives you the strength to make new friends, to venture into new places, and to overcome new obstacles and endure the old.

If God were to stand in front of you and call you a "mighty warrior"—a "strong military wife"—would you react the way Gideon did? "My clan's the weakest ... and I'm the runt of the litter" (Judges 6:15). Would you say, "But God, I'm not strong enough to be a 'strong' military wife. I am barely surviving. I am definitely not thriving. I don't have the strength"?

If that's how you would respond, don't worry. You're exactly where God wants you.

Our Training Must Come from God

About a month after Cliff had left for his deployment, I was in full Great Health Nut mode, visiting the gym daily, working out, and working hard. But some days were harder than others. I noticed that on Mondays I usually was motivated and ready to go, but by the time Wednesdays and Thursdays rolled around, it was more and more difficult to get up and drive myself the couple of miles to work out. So I decided it might be a good idea to enlist the help of a personal trainer. Someone who would spur me on and keep me accountable.

Misty did just that. Left to myself, I would have been content just to walk the treadmill on "manual." But Misty pushed me. Instead of walking, we ran. Instead of ten push-ups, we did twenty. Instead of jogging, we sprinted. Day in and day out, she helped me work harder and push myself longer than I would have done or really even wanted to do. She trained me, over and over, increasing my stamina.

And what happened? I lost weight. I felt better. I got stronger. But before any of that could occur, I had to be trained. That was the other reason for getting a personal trainer. I had no idea how to use most of the equipment in the gym. I needed someone to guide me and show me what to do and how to do it.

Gideon too had no idea how to handle the task before him. There was no training manual on how to be a warrior and take out a bunch of Midianites. But after putting God through some tests and finally becoming convinced that God was indeed the commander of this mission, Gideon mustered as many men as he could find, starting with thirty-two thousand. But if you remember the story, that number was too great. God had Gideon reduce his group down to ten thousand, and then to just three hundred. (See Judges 7.)

Why did God do that to Gideon? Was he trying to make it harder? Did he want Gideon to fail? Or did he want Gideon to rely solely on him? God wants the same for us. When we must rely solely on God, the credit for anything and everything we do goes to him. It's nothing we've done. When someone says, "Oh, you are such a strong woman" because you're a military wife, smile and say, "No, I'm not. But I am God Strong. God's the one who keeps me going. He's the one who carries me." There is no *I* in God Strong. It's all about God.

Just as God gave Gideon the strength and the training to overcome his enemy, God gives us the opportunity to win our battles. He gives us the strength to face our financial problems, troubled relationships, marital struggles, and difficulties with our children. But also just as Gideon was forced to strip away most of the men he had planned to use for his battle, God asks us to strip away what we don't need—our pride, our self-will, our plans, our intentions, and our idea of how things should be.

LEARNING HOW TO PACE

To be God Strong, we can't run ahead of God. We can't run behind him either. We must be in sync with him, and to do that, we have to PACE ourselves (pursue, act, concentrate, encourage). If you run any kind of long-distance races, like 5Ks or marathons, you already know that a pace goal is important if you want to finish well. By figuring out the time you have to run each mile to get the finish time you want, you can run smoothly and steadily instead of attacking the run at full speed and burning out before the finish line.

I've been training for my first 5K and learning what it means to pace myself. I'm a pretty competitive person, so anything I do is usually at one speed: fast. Anything I participate in I try to do at only one level: the best. So pacing myself—slowing down, staying consistent and steady—is a different speed for me. When I'm running on the track, training, and someone runs past me—maybe they're running faster; maybe they've passed me quite a few times—I have to remember that I have my own pace to run. I have my own purpose to accomplish.

PURSUE

When we think about our pace, we must first think about how we pursue God. To pursue means to follow, to strive after, to search for. I can never cross the finish line if I don't ever start the race. I can never experience God's strength if I don't look for it. When we pursue God with our hearts and our minds and everything we have, we embrace what he wants to give us, and that is his peace and his love and his hope. Matthew 24:13 reminds us, "Staying with it—that's what God requires. Stay with it to the end. You won't be sorry, and you'll be saved." When we pursue God, regardless of our circumstances, regardless of how we are feeling, our spiritual foundations are fortified.

ACT

But it's not enough just to be willing to pursue God. We must also be able to act, the second step in keeping pace. I can want with everything I have to finish, but until I move and actually start running the race, I'm never going to see the results, and I'm certainly not going to be closer to the finish line. This can be hard to do if you're already feeling overwhelmed by life. But have you ever started an exercise program, maybe to walk thirty minutes every other day, and noticed how much better you feel if you stick with it for a couple of weeks?

The same is true when you put God first and act in his will. Take a few minutes each day to read his Word, to talk with him and ask him for his guidance and strength. I'm not talking about any kind of formula or ritual you must do. I'm talking about being the kind of military wife who refuses to slump over in a heap but instead is willing to at least stand and keep walking, taking little steps, one foot in front of the other, depending not on herself but on God.

I know what you're thinking. "Read the Bible daily? I can barely find any time at all for myself!" But here's what I've discovered. When something is important enough to us, we *make* the time for it. We also are more willing to make time for things that we enjoy, that we don't feel like we're just checking off on our to-do list.

A couple of years ago, I was feeling convicted that I had never read the Bible from cover to cover. I had read many Christian nonfiction books about important topics in the Bible, but I'd never read the entire Book for myself. When I found myself reading those books and actually skipping over the Scriptures to get to the next part of what the author was saying, I realized I needed a reality check. I decided that my new goal would be to read the Bible from start to finish, and I would read it for enjoyment, at my own speed. I wouldn't try to follow one of the many daily Bible reading plans out there or set a certain number of chapters to get through each day. I'd tried those methods, and they had never worked for me. Instead, I would simply pick up the Bible and read.

I got a copy of *The Message*, which is an easy-to-read paraphrase of the Bible, started in Genesis in November of 2007, and finished Revelation in November of 2008. There were days and sometimes weeks that I wasn't able to read, but there were also days that I couldn't put the Bible down and read many, many chapters at a time. My Bible is filled with underlinings and notes of what I discovered during this quest of reading it through entirely, but I never would have gotten through it if I hadn't first decided to just act. I've now started back at the beginning, hoping to read it through again. This time I'm reading the *NIV Study Bible*, and God is continuing to show me things I hadn't noticed before.

CONCENTRATE

The third step in our pace to be God Strong is to concentrate. When I am running on the track, I have a certain goal I want to accomplish. Maybe it's running a mile without stopping or running that mile within a certain amount of time. I know that if I don't concentrate on my speed, my stride, and my breathing, I might not reach that goal. I might start speeding up and run out of steam too early; I might start thinking about something and get lost in my thoughts and not realize I'm running slower than I need to be. I have to stay focused on what I'm doing. And in life, I have to stay focused on God.

We can often fall into the trap of making comparisons with other people, especially other wives. We start looking at how someone else is doing and we wonder what's wrong with us. Why does *she* look like she has it so together and I don't? We assume that every other military wife in the world is handling everything the way she's supposed to and we're not. We're running the track, but we're not looking ahead of us because we're looking at everyone else. We're not concentrating on what really matters. But here's a secret: every other wife *does not* have it all together!

One of the benefits of being part of a group like Wives of Faith is that you discover very quickly that what you're feeling is not unique. Other women, whether or not they have their husbands home, deal with the same ups and downs, the same trials and challenges, that you do. They have days when they struggle to get everything done, and they have days when they feel like they're doing okay.

I will talk more about this later, but I believe one of the tools Satan uses most is the feeling of loneliness; you feel stuck outside the circle instead of feeling like you belong to a community that loves and cares about you. Loneliness quickly tears away your strength and makes you feel weak and helpless. If we want to avoid it, we must make sure we are concentrating on what God wants us to do and not be concerned with anything or anyone else.

Encourage

That brings us to the last step we need to remember. Encouragement. All of us need encouragement. Just look at all of the different greeting cards we send and the awards we give to recognize people for doing good and exceptional things. All of us need a gentle push of inspiration from time to time, a reminder that what we are doing is valued. But how often do we do that for ourselves?

When do you tell yourself you're doing a good job? That you are meeting your challenges well and doing the best you can with the circumstances you are in? How much more often do you put yourself down? "I'm hopeless." "I can't do anything right." "I'm so stupid." "I'm so ugly." "I'm such a failure."

In her book *Knit Together*, Debbie Macomber calls this kind of talk negative self-talk and reminds us that it has no place in our lives.[3] You would never use those kinds of words with a friend, so why would you use them on yourself? Instead, we need to turn those negative and discouraging thoughts into encouraging and uplifting words that will keep us going. "I am doing a great job taking one day at a time." "I'm so proud of myself for fixing that leak!" "This week will be hard, but with God's help, I'm going to get through it!"

Psychologist Dr. Henry H. Goddard performed experiments to measure fatigue in children by hooking them up to a special measuring device called an ergograph. After someone told a tired child he was doing fine, the child's energy curve on the machine soared. But if someone gave that same child discouraging words or pointed out what he was doing wrong, it had the opposite effect.[4]

When I work out, I've noticed that when I'm getting tired and slowing down, ready to quit, if I start telling myself, "You can do it," "Just a little longer; keep going!" or, "Don't give up; you're almost there!" I am much more likely to keep going than if I allow myself to think, "You're not going to make it," "You should have stayed home today," or, "This is too hard; just give up!"

The same thing happens in life. We need to encourage ourselves as military wives with our words, with the books we read, the music we listen to, the shows we watch. Especially when we are feeling tired and worn out.

Another kind of encouragement we need to invest in as we pace ourselves is to encourage others. I always feel so much better when I'm helping someone else feel better too. In part this is because when I'm thinking of someone else, I'm thinking less about myself. You can encourage someone with just a simple smile, a supportive email, or a phone call. There are so many things you can do that can be an enormous blessing to others.

OUR ULTIMATE SUPPORT

God will hold us up if we lean on him. Isaiah 50:11 reminds us, "For anyone out there who doesn't know where you're going, anyone groping in the dark, here's what: Trust in GOD. *Lean* on your God!"

Relying on God's strength means accepting that our own isn't enough and that it was never intended to be enough.

When my son was first learning to walk, he had to figure out the whole concept of balance and leg coordination. It was easier for him when he could hold my hand or his dad's hand. As he took step after step, he could lean on us for support. He could compensate for his wobbles and accidental trips with the stability and firmness of his parent walking next to him. When he was about to fall, my hand would help him find his balance once again. God does the same for us. His steadiness keeps us stable. His permanence helps us endure. His strength supports us. He is the one who makes us strong.

STRENGTH BUILDERS

"Exercise daily in God—no spiritual flabbiness, please! Workouts in the gymnasium are useful, but a disciplined life in God is far more so, making you fit both today and forever" (1 Timothy 4:8).

"It was a case of Christ's strength moving in on my weakness. Now I take limitations in stride, and with good cheer, these limitations that cut me down to size—abuse, accidents, opposition, bad breaks. I just let Christ take over! And so the weaker I get, the stronger I become" (2 Corinthians 12:9–10).

"While we were children, our parents did what *seemed* best to them. But God is doing what *is* best for us, training us to live God's holy best. At the time, discipline isn't much fun. It always feels like it's going against the grain. Later, of course, it pays off handsomely, for it's the well-trained who find themselves mature in their relationship with God" (Hebrews 12:11).

"If you grasp and cling to life on your terms, you'll lose it, but if you let that life go, you'll get life on God's terms" (Luke 17:33).

STRENGTH TRAINERS

1. In what areas of your life do you feel weak? What do you usually try to do to compensate for those weaknesses? What should you do?

2. Where has Me Strength interfered with your attempts to rely on God? In order to be God Strong, what must happen?

3. Think of one struggle that you're dealing with and apply the PACE principles to it. How can you *pursue* God through this? How will you *act*? What must you do to fully *concentrate* on him? In what ways can you find *encouragement* as you deal with this challenge?

CHAPTER THREE

FEAR BLOCKS MY FOCUS

★ ★ ★ ★ ★

MY BEDROOM WAS DARK except for the faint glow coming through the doorway from the clock radio I kept in my bathroom. I glanced at the clock next to my bed: 1:04 a.m. What woke me up? Then I heard him. Our miniature schnauzer, Sammy, was standing at the end of my bed, his growl stern and very loud in the quiet of the house. Through the dim light, I could see that his back was arched, his muscles tense, and his eyes staring at the open door leading into the hall. *He sees something*, I thought. *Or someone.*

Cliff was in Iraq and I was by myself. Now my muscles were tense. Was there someone in the house? Our son was asleep in his room on the other end of the house. Was he okay? My cell phone was on the opposite side of the room. There was nothing to grab to defend myself against an intruder; my Bible was the only thing on my bedside table. *I know God calls it our sword of truth, but would he have a problem if I tried to really use it like a sword—or at least threw it?*

I took a deep breath and listened, but I didn't hear anything except the pounding of my heart. I didn't take my eyes off Sammy, and he wasn't taking his eyes off the door. Suddenly, he backed up, whimpering. *What kind of watchdog are you?* I thought as my blood raced and I got ready to confront whatever or whoever was coming into my room … only to turn and face my seven-year-old. For whatever reason, he had lingered a little longer outside the door than he usually did when he got up in the middle of the night.

As I breathed a huge sigh of relief and walked Caleb back to his room, I shook my head at my "brave" dog. Glad it wasn't a real intruder!

One of the biggest fears I often struggle with is sleeping in the house alone when my husband is gone. It doesn't matter if it's during a weekend drill, training, or a full-term deployment, I do not like sleeping in that big bed by myself! At night, I can hear every creak and groan of the house, and of course in the darkness they all seem a hundred times louder and there are a hundred scary possibilities of what they could be. I was that way as a child, often peering into the dark closet in my bedroom at night and imagining that there were all sorts of scary monsters hiding in there to get me.

I know we live on a safe street in a very safe neighborhood and that our house is good and secure. But when my mind starts wandering at night, as it sometimes will, my imagination can get the best of me, and every *CSI* and *Criminal Minds* episode I've ever seen starts replaying over and over in my mind!

Most of us wrestle with fear throughout our lives. Whether irrational or well founded, our fears can block us from what we want to do or where we want to go. They can be simple annoyances or paralyzing ones. One of the greatest dangers of giving in to our fears and allowing them room in our lives is that if a fear is there, faith isn't.

If I fear that my husband will get hurt or, worse, killed, then I've stopped trusting that God is in control and that he is with my husband. If I fear that the bills are piling up and wonder how in the world we're going to pay the mortgage at the end of the month, then I've stopped believing the words of Isaiah 41:10: "Don't panic. I'm with you. There's no need to fear for I'm your God. I'll give you strength. I'll help you. I'll hold you steady, keep a firm grip on you."

Imagine that your heart has a window, and that through this window you can see the direction God has laid out for you, the plan he has for you and for your family. The view he's given you is a beautiful one, and it's exciting because you know God's presence is there and he's the one who has given you this incredible view. But suddenly, a thick, black steel bar appears. Then another, and another, until your window is now almost covered. Suddenly, you're not even trying to look out the window. You're just looking at bars. You're looking at fear.

This is what fear does to us. It blocks our focus and dismantles our confidence. Instead of allowing rays of light, which represent God's love and his plan, to shine through, these bars of fear block out that light, keeping a constant barrier between us and God.

What are the bars of fear you're facing today? Change? Losing your husband? Losing a child? Being alone? Starting over? Being rejected? Experiencing disappointment? Everything going wrong?

One of the things I fear will sound a little silly, but I don't like walking over a grate or a manhole cover in the road. It's an irrational fear, I know, but anytime I see a manhole cover, I step over it or walk around it. My husband teases me a lot over this. "You know, cars and trucks drive over these things!" he tells me, pointing out that it's highly unlikely I'm going to step on one and fall in. Of course, I know he's right, but still, I can't bring myself to step on one of those things. I know that the road around the grate is solid; I don't know if the grate is. But if I believe that the grate will hold when one-ton cars and trucks drive over it, then shouldn't I believe that the grate will hold me? And if I believe that God looks out for others (and I must, if I pray for other people), then shouldn't I believe that he will look out for me as well? So why do I fear?

In Mark 9, a man brings his demon-possessed son to Jesus for healing. This father had been through so much. Can you imagine how helpless he must have felt, forced to stand by and watch his son thrashing around, unable to speak, sometimes unable to move? In verse 17, the man explains to Jesus that the disciples had already tried to heal the boy but, for whatever reason, could not. Read what Jesus and the man discuss, starting in verse 21.

> He asked the boy's father, "How long has this been going on?"
>
> "Ever since he was a little boy. Many times it pitches him into fire or the river to do away with him. If you can do anything, do it. Have a heart and help us!"
>
> Jesus said, "If? There are no 'ifs' among believers. Anything can happen."
>
> No sooner were the words out of his mouth than the father cried, "Then I believe. Help me with my doubts!"
>
> —Mark 9:21–24

This is such a poignant scene of a father's desperate cry for help, and it's not just a plea to help his son; he implores Jesus to help him with his faith as well. Faith isn't something we can manufacture on our own; it's a gift we receive from God (Ephesians 2:8). Faith is the opposite of fear. We adopt complete trust in and dependence on God. We *believe* that he will do what he says he will. And when we doubt, we ask God to help remove those doubts, ensuring that our windows of focus stay clear. The father was willing to trade his fears for the faith that Jesus could restore his son.

The first time I started thinking about what it means to trade my fears for faith happened when I started attending a women's Bible study. We were going through Jennifer Rothschild's *Walking by Faith*, and in the video, Rothschild talks about trading fear for faith. As I drove home afterward, I thought about all of the fears I had. I feared the unknown because my husband was just a couple of months away from deploying for the first time. I feared not meeting a writing deadline. And the list went on.

Still driving home, I decided I should pray about my fears. *Lord*, I prayed silently, *help me trade my faith for fear.* Wait a minute, that wasn't right! I chuckled, as I said out loud, "Lord, help me trade my *fear* for *faith*!" That was better.

I continued to pray out loud, trading each specific fear for a faith that God would provide. "I trade my fear of Cliff's deployment for the faith that you will be there for me. I trade my fear of failing for the faith that you will help me succeed."

As I continued to pray, I realized something incredible had happened. While I had been praying, it had started to rain. Hard! Normally, I hate driving in rain, because I am always afraid the car will hydroplane. But during this particular storm, I hadn't even noticed it was raining. My hands weren't clenched around the steering wheel; my muscles weren't tense. I was absolutely relaxed and happy. The Holy Spirit had done a work right there in the car, taking away my fears, even the fear of driving in the rain, which I didn't pray about, and gave to me in place of those fears the gifts of faith, trust, comfort, and wholeness.

When we focus everything we have on God, we aren't distracted by doubts and fears. Think about new parents with their first child. When our son was a baby, whenever we sat down for a meal, our focus was always on him. We weren't looking at him just because he was so darn cute (which he was). We were absolutely overwhelmed by love for him, so much so that it was hard to take our eyes off of him. Our love kept our focus where it needed to be. That is the same kind of focus God wants us to have on him. It's the same focus he has on us.

CHOOSING FAITH OVER FEAR

Have you ever noticed how often the words "fear not" appear in the Bible? Lloyd Ogilvie, former pastor of First Presbyterian Church in Hollywood and former chaplain for the US Senate, once noted that there are 366 "fear not" verses in the Bible. John Ortberg, in his book *If You Want to Walk on Water, You've Got to Get out of the Boat*, points out that the reason God says "fear not" so much isn't because God wants us to be spared from feeling afraid. Ortberg writes, "I think God says 'fear not' so often because fear is the number one reason human beings are tempted to avoid doing what God asks them to do."[5] I believe that God has a special purpose for each of us who are called military wives. We have an incredible opportunity to be blessings to our families, to our sister military wives, and to the communities in which we live and work. But many of us are still at the starting line because of our fears. Some of us have made it around a couple of laps but have slowed down because of fear.

In Matthew 25:14 – 30, Jesus tells the story of a rich man who had to leave for a business trip and left his money under the watchful eye of the men who worked for him. Each of the three men received a portion of the money according to what their boss thought they could handle. While he was away, two of his employees were able to double what he had entrusted to them. But the other employee played it safe; instead of working like the others to increase what was given to him, he hid it away. He feared he might fail, so he refused to take a risk. And as a result, what was given to him ultimately was taken away and given to someone else.

Sometimes our fears actually induce the very failures we fear and try to avoid. We convince ourselves to choose the easy instead of the hard, the good instead of the great, the standard instead of the best. We survive, but we do nothing that might help us thrive, because we fear the risk and we fear what it might mean if we don't succeed. We really don't want to find out.

Being afraid of failing is like shopping in a department store and seeing a beautiful vase on the very top shelf. You would love to see it more closely, but you're not sure if it's worth standing on your tiptoes for. You might look silly to the other customers. Besides, what if you reach for it and it slips out of your fingers and you break it? You're not even sure how much it costs; it's probably more than you want to pay, anyway. You talk yourself out of even trying and you walk on. You'll never know that the vase you were eyeing actually was free. You only had to reach up and take it.

How often do you allow fear to keep you from doing something? Do you resist meeting new people because you fear you won't hit it off? Do you avoid getting involved with your FRG (family readiness group) or your local military wives club because you don't want to commit to something you may not like or, worse, to go somewhere you may get hurt? Do you refuse to think about (or plan for) your husband's approaching deployment because you believe that if you ignore it, it will just go away?

God doesn't want us to fear! He wants us to have faith. He wants us to believe him and trust him when he tells us *not* to fear. In John 12:24 Jesus talks about how a grain of wheat will never be more than just a seed unless that seed is buried and allowed to sprout and reproduce over and over. In verse 25, he says, "In the same way, anyone who holds on to life just as it is destroys that life. But if you let it go, reckless in your love, you'll have it forever, real and eternal." Our lives weren't meant to be the same as when we started. We have to release our fears in order to see where God wants to take us. We have to let our fears go.

For one brief instant, Peter released his fears when he stepped out of the boat to meet Jesus on the water. Picture the scene: it was around four o'clock in the morning, still dark, with perhaps just a hint of light coming in around the edges of the horizon. The wind had picked up considerably, and the boat the disciples were in was being tossed, at the mercy of the fierce gusts. But then, they see him. Jesus is coming to them from across the water. And he's not swimming; he's walking! And Peter, impulsive Peter, right away asks to join him. "Master, if it's really you, call me to come to you on the water" (Matthew 14:28). And when Jesus says, "Come," Peter jumps out boldly and walks on the water to join him.

But then it happens. Out of the corner of his eye, Peter sees the waves that are crashing below him. He looks down. He feels the strong winds pushing his body around. He looks out and sees the dark clouds rolling. No longer is he focused on Jesus; fear has his attention now.

As military wives, I think we can relate to what Peter was experiencing.

Peter feared drowning. We fear losing our identities.

Peter grew anxious over the churning waves that threatened him. We feel overwhelmed by the rapid changes we sometimes (and often) must deal with.

Peter feared the forceful winds flying in his face, stinging his eyes, almost stealing his breath. We fear losing control.

What I believe Peter feared the most, however, was missing that moment with Jesus. This is what we should fear as well.

REMEMBER TIMES GOD WAS AT WORK

We often find it easier to *say* we need to focus on God, to trust God, than actually to do it. Madeleine L'Engle tells the story of a father who loved his son dearly and wanted to protect him from the hurts and fears of the world. So he constantly told his son that no one could be trusted. L'Engle writes, "One evening when the father came home, his son came running down the stairs to greet him, and the

Survival Sisters
Facing Fear

I've been an Army wife for almost twenty-one years, and the word *fear* conjures up many memories and feelings for me. Fear of losing my soldier and best friend, fear of how his experiences will change him, fear of how the kids will handle the deployments, fear that I can't handle single parenting and all the challenges by myself, fear our marriage is not strong enough to handle all the stress. The list can go on and on if I allow my mind to go there, but God's Word is clear. Joshua 1:9: "Have I not commanded you? Be strong and courageous. Do not be terrified; do not be discouraged, for the LORD your God will be with you wherever you go" (NIV).

These are the words that bring me comfort whenever my husband is away. They brought me comfort when I watched and heard a mortar attack happening in real time on the webcam. They calmed me down as I watched the news and as the death count continued to rise in Iraq. They gave me assurance when my teenagers were acting out because Dad was away again and he missed another [fill in the blank]. They were the same words that helped me when I was awakened by loud noises outside, and when my husband arrived home safely and our family dynamics were different and readjusting was hard.

The Lord commanded me to be strong, courageous, and not to be terrified or discouraged (all the emotions I was feeling) but to remember that the Lord my God was with us just as he was with my husband in another country or simply away for training!

The Lord is with us wherever we are, and his Word brings us much comfort in an unmanageable world. The deployments probably will continue, the challenges and trials will be different, but the Lord is the same today, tomorrow, and forever. He will never leave us or forsake us. He strengthens us during those difficult times when we are weak.

— *Melissa Kuhlman,*
Army wife

father stopped him at the landing. 'Son,' he said, 'Daddy has taught you that people are not to be trusted, hasn't he?' 'Yes, Daddy.' 'You can't trust anybody, can you?' 'No, Daddy.' 'But you can trust Daddy, can't you?' 'Oh, yes, Daddy.' The father then held out his arms and said, 'Jump,' and the little boy jumped with absolute trust that his father's arms were waiting for him. But the father stepped aside and let the little boy fall crashing to the floor. 'You see,' he said to his son, 'you must trust *no*body.'"[6]

This story broke my heart when I read it, but I wonder how many women — as little girls — had fathers, mothers, or others they trusted who broke that trust in one way or another. Instead of catching them, they dropped them. Instead of teaching them to trust, they took that trust completely away.

You may find it difficult to trust and not fear; disappointment and hurt may have been like extended relatives who have come for a visit and can't take the hint that they've overstayed their welcome. But it's so important that you know that God is good. That he is strong. And that he can be trusted. Let's talk about why.

Hebrews 13:6 tells us we can be fearless because we have God by our side. We can believe in his love, in his help, and in his hope. Especially when we remember the moments we have already seen them.

Whenever I found myself struggling during my husband's almost year-long deployment, I forced myself to go back to a time four years earlier, when I was standing on a curb in front of the Nashville airport, waiting. My photographer and I were supposed to be getting on a plane to the Middle East to cover stories of what God was doing in the lives of sailors aboard an aircraft carrier the first week of the Iraq war. The only problem was that our trip had been bumped up a day early, and my passport had still not arrived. There was a great possibility that I would not be getting on that plane.

I had not looked for this trip, and so when the opportunity presented itself, I had approached it from a "great if it happens, okay if it doesn't" point of view. But being so close to going yet still without a passport in my hands, I bowed my head and silently prayed. *God, I know that you are in control. I ask that you make a way, that whatever happens makes it obvious and without any doubt that you are leading this trip.* As I said "amen," my phone rang. The airport's post office was calling. They had my passport and would bring it around to me. We made it on the plane with just five minutes to spare.

That is one example of how I've seen God work in my life in a miraculous way. I've also seen him work in the lives of others. In one week, just a couple of days apart, I received emails from two different women. One was the wife of a reservist; one was the wife of an active duty soldier. The reservist wife's husband was home; the active duty wife's husband was in Iraq. Both of these precious women were young and had small children, and both of them had just been told by their husbands that they wanted out of their marriages.

Both wives emailed me through Wives of Faith, seeking prayer and a listening ear. I passed on their prayer requests to the other ladies in our leadership team, and we began to pray. Hard. For each woman and for her husband. After a few months of praying for these ladies, we invited them both to attend our first weekend conference, and by the time the conference was held, both husbands had come back to their wives, seeking forgiveness and a fresh start.

Kelly emailed me shortly before the conference with a good report on how things were going. She told me that for months, friends and family had all been encouraging her to leave her husband. "I finally told them that I pray to God every day to restore my marriage, and kicking him out or wishing that he would leave would be turning my back on God's help, and I will not give up on this fight. Being a military wife is definitely not for everyone. I am just so very happy that I turned to God in my time of need instead of pushing him away. Maybe this was his plan all along, to bring me back to him."

When fear tries to steal our focus, we can get our focus back by looking at God's amazing works—in others and in ourselves—and use these reminders to help jog our memories of what God has done and the promise of what he can do.

FINE-TUNING OUR FOCUS

Pursuing God is another way we overcome our fears and fine-tune our focus. We mentioned this in the last chapter when we talked about how to pace ourselves. But there's nothing quick about pursuing God. We're talking more marathon than sprint. We run after God regardless of how much we trip over our feet and fall.

Restoring our focus on God can also take place when we get quiet before him. This can be hard at times, because when we get quiet, we have a better chance to process our thoughts, and sometimes we don't always like facing what we need to think about. When we're quiet, we can better hear the beating of our hearts and we feel a little more vulnerable. We remember feelings we're used to pushing away. We don't always like being quiet and vulnerable, because military wives are supposed to be strong and resilient.

Remember what I said about being in church and struggling with the tears? Many of us at one time or another feel like we can't approach God unless we're feeling good, being good, or even looking good. I am here to say don't ever feel that way again! I believe that God uses our tears to get our attention and our *focus*. Our tears become a transmitter that the Holy Spirit can work through to minister to our hearts, to help shed our fears, and to restore wholeness to our souls.

So how is our belief in God able to outweigh any fears that may be lying dormant, in between the worries and stresses of life? Here's how:

Because God doesn't leave (Isaiah 41:10).

Because God uses the ordinary to create the extraordinary (John 12:24–25).

Because we can't see our fears any more than we can see God, but we can see God's love and care and handiwork everywhere we turn. Our fears can reside only in the troubled and worried crevices of our hearts. But God can remove those troubles (John 14:11–14).

Because we can see and hear the testimonies of those who traded their fears for faith, including Noah, Abraham, Sarah, Daniel, Peter, and Paul (see Hebrews 11).

Fear is not a natural part of our existence; at least, it wasn't part of God's original plan. Only after Adam and Eve sinned did fear enter the picture (Genesis 3:10). So why do we let fear have so much freedom in our lives? Look what author and evangelist E. Stanley Jones has to say about fear:

> I am inwardly fashioned for faith, not for fear. Fear is not my native land; faith is. I am so made that worry and anxiety are sand in the machinery of life; faith is the oil. I live better by faith and confidence than by fear, doubt and anxiety. In anxiety and worry, my being is gasping for breath — these are not my native air. But in faith and confidence, I breathe freely — these are my native air. A Johns Hopkins University doctor says, "We do not know why it is that worriers die sooner than the non-worriers, but that is a fact." But I, who am simple of mind, think I know; we are inwardly constructed in nerve and tissue, brain cell and soul, for faith and not for fear. God made us that way. To live by worry is to live against reality.[7]

When we replace our fears with faith that God is in control, we underscore our trust and our belief in God's power and his strength. We can be like Abraham: when we feel like everything is hopeless, we can believe anyway, living not on the basis of what we can't do but on the basis of what God says he will do (Romans 4:18).

Strength Builders

"Be prepared. You're up against far more than you can handle on your own. Take all the help you can get, every weapon God has issued, so that when it's all over but the shouting you'll still be on your feet" (Ephesians 6:13).

"Don't panic. I'm with you. There's no need to fear for I'm your God. I'll give you strength. I'll help you. I'll hold you steady, keep a firm grip on you" (Isaiah 41:10).

"When everything was hopeless, Abraham believed anyway, deciding to live not on the basis of what he saw he *couldn't* do but on what God said he *would* do" (Romans 4:18).

"God is there, ready to help; I'm fearless no matter what. Who or what can get to me?" (Hebrews 13:6).

Strength Trainers

1. Why do we struggle so much with fear?

2. How does fear affect your walk with God?

3. What are the fears you struggle with the most? Take some time to be very honest with yourself. Make a list and write them down. Ask God to help you trade those fears for the faith that he will meet your needs.

CHAPTER FOUR

I Am
Not Alone

★ ★ ★ ★ ★

ONE OF THE HARDEST EMOTIONS we face living the military life is loneliness. After all, a beautiful blessing of marriage is having someone by your side. You don't have to face life on your own; you have someone to walk with and to face problems and adversity with.

But when your husband is in the military, no matter what branch or type, there are many times you find yourself alone and facing those problems by yourself. As I write this, my husband is away for a drill weekend. Rain is pelting down outside my window, and all I can think about is how nice it would be if he were home and we could curl up on the couch and watch a movie together. I'm not really feeling loneliness right now; I know he'll be home tomorrow night. Maybe it is more of a longing because I miss my husband. But longing has a lot to do with feeling lonely too.

There is a difference between being lonely and being alone. There are times when it is good to be by ourselves, to take a moment for rest, or to read, or to be quiet with our thoughts, or to pray. There are several instances in the Bible when Jesus went away to be alone for these reasons. Only when we don't necessarily want to be by ourselves can loneliness overtake our souls and wrap around our hearts. We were not meant to lead solitary lives. God made that point when he created Eve for Adam. He said, "It is not good for the man to be alone" (Genesis 2:18 NIV). Adam needed someone, just as you and I need someone. But when that someone is in the military, well, as you have probably already found, your needs are usually not the priority.

Melissa is an Army wife whose husband is in Special Forces and has frequent deployments. When I first met her, she struck me as very confident and a strong, self-reliant military wife, someone who is used to the ups and downs of deployments. But she too struggles with loneliness. As she was preparing for her husband to leave on another deployment, she emailed me and told me how she dreads those lonely nights: "I think what has helped me the most is finding others in the same situation. We have had Bible studies in our homes, met for coffee, or spent hours on the phone at night, drinking herbal tea and chatting about life and kids. (After our children are in bed, of course!) It's hard to explain loneliness to those who have never experienced it."

If you have been where Melissa is, then you know: loneliness can be an unsettling quiet that screams loudly into your ears that something is missing. You can feel lost and disconnected from everything you hold dear.

Right in Front of Us

We can be alone and still feel whole when we rely on God's strength to fill in the missing pieces of our hearts or lives. Unfortunately, that generally isn't what we do. God is often the last one we turn to, and the more we struggle against being alone, the lonelier we can feel.

Survival Sisters
Never Alone

Throughout my deployment, God continually showed me how strong I could be because his loving arms are my strength. Whenever I started to get depressed or loneliness started to take its toll, God always reminded me that he never leaves me or forsakes me. I really learned to hold on to that promise like never before.

I had mowed the grass all summer and was doing well at it too. The yard looked great. I felt confident and had convinced myself I had this deployment under control. My confidence fell to the ground, though, when one day the lawn mower decided not to start. I instantly felt alone and confused: how was I going to start this stupid piece of lawn equipment without my husband home to assist me the second I was in need? I called some friends to ask what I should do, and they tried their best to give advice, but nothing I tried worked. I said, "Thanks anyway," and hung up the phone.

It was such a simple task, but I felt totally defeated. I started to sob as I sat on the seat of my green John Deer tractor. Then I started to pray. "Lord, please ease my frustration and help get this lawn mower started. I feel so alone."

About five minutes later, my friends called back and told me they were on their way to my house and would be there in about twenty minutes. The feeling of defeat was totally swept away. God knew I was at the point where I felt I couldn't take any more! He never left me and even provided an answer to my prayer.

— *Kristi Reid,*
Marine Reserve wife

This morning, I decided to give Sammy, our dog, a treat. Since he's been bad lately about not eating his food (and just wanting treats), instead of handing him the treat directly, I buried it underneath his food in his bowl. Even though Sammy stood there and watched me do it, he still didn't eat it right away. That's because he couldn't find it! He cocked his head and looked at the bowl, and then under the bowl; where did that treat go? He went around the bowl and then started looking around the room, still trying to find the treat and ignoring the bowl of food, his main source of nutrition and nourishment. If he had just started eating what was readily available to him, he would have discovered the treat just below the surface, and well within his reach.

That is often what we do when we're lonely, isn't it? We look everywhere, trying to find the solution to our aching hearts, everywhere but to God. And though we may not be able to see him, he is there, well within our reach. He wants to remove our struggles and sorrows and replace them with joy and gladness.

So if we know all of that, if we are aware of the goodness and the greatness of God, then why do we still struggle with being alone? This is a battle that has gone on for a long time, a fight between holding on to our human nature and embracing God's nature.

With our human nature, we say, "What did I do to deserve this?" With God's nature, we say, "What is God doing in this?"

With human nature, we think, "I am weak because I am alone." With God's nature, we remember, "I am weak but God is strong. And I am not alone."

With human nature, we wish desperately for the loneliness to end. When we apply God's nature to our lives, we hold fast to the promise that he never leaves. We put away being Me Strong and we realize what it means to be God Strong.

Look at what Romans 8:5–8 says: "Those who think they can do it on their own end up obsessed with measuring their own moral muscle but never get around to exercising it in real life. Those who trust God's action in them find that God's Spirit is in them—living and breathing God! Obsession with self in these matters is a dead end; attention to God leads us out into the open, into a spacious, free life. Focusing on the self is the opposite of focusing on God. Anyone completely absorbed in self ignores God, ends up thinking more about self than God. That person ignores who God is and what he is doing. And God isn't pleased at being ignored."

When we are dealing with situations of loneliness—and deployment is a prime example—our human nature wants to focus inward. We want to shout, "But what about *my* needs, *my* feelings, and *my* hurts?" God wants to use these heart pains to get us to look up! He wants us to realize that he is meeting our needs, that he understands our feelings and holds our hurts in his hands.

Go back to that last passage in Romans: "Those *who trust God's action in them* find that God's Spirit is in them" (emphasis mine). When we take ourselves out of the way and allow God to work amid our feelings of emptiness or isolation, the Holy Spirit takes over, bringing calm to our chaos and contentment to our discontent. In the New International Version, Romans 8:6 says that "the mind controlled by the Spirit is life and peace." Wouldn't you like to be able to experience peace when you're by yourself? No more fretting, no more struggle? The key is to know daily where your focus lies. We must remember what Jesus went through for us and that he has experienced everything we have—except for sinning—and we must do as the author of Hebrews says: "Let's walk right up to him and get what he is so ready to give. Take the mercy, accept the help." (See Hebrews 4:14–16.)

AVOIDING SELF-PITY

Talk about feeling lonely! Naomi's husband and both of her sons had died. And now she was sending her daughters-in-law away. Ruth and Orpah had been loyal to her, but Naomi knew that they were still young and that the possibility of remarrying and having children remained an option for them both. Not so with Naomi. She was now well on in years; there was no possibility of having more children. She would be alone for the rest of her days.

Naomi could feel the emptiness in her heart, and she couldn't help but taste the bitterness of her situation; it was hard to see the good in anything anymore. So what that Ruth had refused to leave and was coming with her back to Judah? Who cared that the whole town of Bethlehem came out to welcome her back when they arrived? Naomi was beyond consolation. Read what she said after she and Ruth arrived back in her hometown: "'Don't call me Naomi,' she told them. 'Call me Mara, because the Almighty has made my life very bitter. I went away full, but the LORD has brought me back empty. Why call me Naomi? The LORD has afflicted me; the Almighty has brought misfortune upon me'" (Ruth 1:20–21 NIV).

Naomi was certainly looking inward at this point in her life. Even with Ruth by her side, she felt alone, abandoned by those she had loved the most, including God. Self-pity had taken over.

Susie Larson, in her book *Alone in Marriage*, writes that "everyone needs to step off the beaten path for a bit and acknowledge that life gets hard sometimes. But in our acknowledgment, we must never forget that *God is always good*, and He asks us to look up. Self-pity is always bad, and requires that we look down."[8] God *is* always good, and it's important to remember that, especially when we're struggling. I don't believe God takes our husbands away for deployments or other reasons just to torment us or to make things hard for us. He is not out to punish us. He wants to love us, and he wants us to love him in return. Just as God has a purpose for my husband as he serves his country, so he has a purpose for me and where I am as I serve in our marriage, our home, our church, and the other callings God has put on my life.

More often than we should, however, we place our hope, trust, and security in our husbands instead of in God. There's a term for this—relational idolatry, an act of placing the responsibility for my well-being on any relationship other than the one I have with God. When I expect that my husband will be the one to make me happy, I expect he will solve all my problems and meet all of my needs. But if we see our husbands as the sole source of our happiness, then when they are away from us, focused on the mission they've been assigned—well, there goes our hope, trust, and security. And in walks self-pity.

There's another part of Naomi's story that we need to look at—Ruth's part.

Here is a woman who also had reason to be sad. After all, she'd lost her husband, the man she had expected to have children with and to grow old with. Now she was a widow. But unlike her mother-in-law, Naomi, she didn't say, "There is nothing left for me." She didn't turn around and go home. Instead, she looked up. "Where you go I will go, and where you stay I will stay. Your people will be my people and your God my God," she told Naomi (Ruth 1:16 NIV).

Ruth certainly wasn't choosing the easy road; she was a Moabite, and Moabites and Judahites did not get along.[9] So by choosing to go home to Judah with Naomi, Ruth was taking a chance that her own loneliness might increase. Still, she wanted to follow God—Naomi's God—and so she decided to go.

Once she got there, she didn't sit down on the couch and wonder where her life was going now. She got up! She went out! Ruth 2:2 tells us that she offered to go out to the fields to pick up leftover grain for their meals. Ruth knew she had two choices: she could give in to her circumstances, or she could make the most of them and embrace the place where God had put her.

This is what we must do when we are faced with a season of being alone. We can't let our loneliness turn into a season of self-pity; instead, we must treat it as a time of growth, a moment for renewal, and a period of hope for the joys to come.

AVOIDING TEMPTATION

When we fall into loneliness, we can find ourselves tripping over traps and temptations if we're not careful. Ever practice retail therapy? Some ladies believe shopping is good for the soul, but it certainly can be bad for your checking account! Spending out of emotion instead of necessity can make things harder in the long run and leave you feeling worse.

I have heard too many stories of women who, while their husbands were away, filled up their time by buying anything and everything they wanted to in order to push out the pain of being alone, only to have to face the bigger pain of explaining to their husbands how they have put their families on the brink of bankruptcy. (Not to mention possibly getting their husbands reprimanded or, worse, on the receiving end of disciplinary action, since the military frowns on service members getting into excessive debt.)

What about overeating? While many women work to lose weight when they are on their own, others seem to gain it, giving in to too many late nights with Ben & Jerry's or making fast food their family's main food source. Eating too much may seem like a minor temptation compared with others, but it can still have consequences—for your budget, for your waistline, even for your health. Struggles with weight can often be the result of allowing our feelings to dictate our actions, keeping our focus inward instead of upward.

When I can, I like to visit message boards and see what military wives are talking about. Many of these women don't claim to have a relationship with God, and as someone who has tried to be committed to my marriage and my family, reading their messages is a reality check for me, particularly when it comes to temptation. Sexual temptation and sexual sin are costing our military marriages a great deal.

In recent a survey by the *Navy Times*, 80 percent of those who responded said they believe that divorce "happens a lot" or is "rampant" within the military community.[10] This shouldn't come as a surprise since divorce is prevalent in our society. When you add the extra stressors of frequent deployments and long absences, staying in a military marriage can be very difficult, whether you have a relationship with God or not. But it's better when you do, as many wives I meet through Wives of Faith tell me. "I don't know how I could do this without God's help" is the statement I often hear from them. And I totally agree!

But just because we know God doesn't mean we won't be tempted. Jesus himself was tempted when he was alone (Matthew 4). And I don't think it is just coincidence that one of the few military wives mentioned in the Bible was caught up in one of the most scandalous acts of temptation, desire, and deceit recorded in the Scriptures.

Bathsheba's husband, Uriah, was a soldier in King David's army. He had been deployed in the field with his men for a while, long enough to have "destroyed the Ammonites and besieged Rabbah" (2 Samuel 11:1 NIV). I'm sure Bathsheba was lonely and missed her husband, just as we are lonely and miss our husbands when they are away from us. The moon was sitting high in the sky one night when Bathsheba decided to slip into a bath, probably wanting to soak away some of the stresses of her day.

Houses during that time often had rooms which were very small and dark — one reason that the courtyards and the flat roofs of those houses were so important. In addition to food preparation and sewing, bathing was done on the roof, and that's probably where Bathsheba took her bath, something that was not considered out of the ordinary in that day.[11] I make that point only because so often Bathsheba seems to be blamed for the immodesty of bathing outside in the first place, but in fact, she was probably not doing anything wrong. But that's when it happened. King David, who apparently couldn't sleep (we're told he "got up from his bed" [2 Samuel 11:2 NIV]), maybe suffering a little guilt for being back at the palace when he was supposed to be out on the battlefield with his men, decided to go up to his roof and get some fresh air. Gazing out over the neighborhood, he saw her, this beautiful woman taking a bath.

He could have looked away, but he didn't. He could have gone back to bed, but instead, he asked a messenger to find out who the woman was. And then once he knew—that she was the wife of a man who was putting his life on the line at that exact moment for him and for his kingdom—David had her brought to him so he could sleep with her.

If you look at the circumstances, it's hard to say that Bathsheba was at fault for the affair. Certainly David held more of the blame. Some commentaries I've read said it would have been hard as a woman in that day to refuse any wish from a king. The Bible doesn't say how much Bathsheba protested or whether she did at all. But we see accounts of other women in biblical times who did the right thing when it was required of them and who stood up for what was right when the men around them were unwilling to do so or were making wrong choices. (Deborah and Jael come to mind [Judges 4], and Abigail [1 Samuel 25].) Still, I have to wonder how much loneliness played a role in Bathsheba's part of the situation, and I have to wonder how loved she felt by a husband who consistently put his men ahead of her, the obligation of a good soldier. We see this when Uriah refused to come home and see her even when David commanded him to, preferring to stay with his men instead. Of course, we know that David was trying to cover up his sin, but Uriah's actions may also shed a little light on what Bathsheba was feeling when she was summoned to the palace; she wasn't a priority for her husband.

If there is anything we can learn from Bathsheba's story, it's that temptation can come to us; we don't necessarily have to go looking for it. But we still must be on guard against it. This is one reason why I am very careful not to put myself in situations that might open the door for temptation, like spending a lot of time with guy friends who aren't my husband. I know several women with male friends who insist they are just friends, but if your husband is away, and you look for support and comfort from another man, regardless of his friendship status, there is a risk it can turn into more than you were planning on.

You may not have a bathtub up on your roof, but you probably have a web browser. Guard your heart against sin that tries to creep in through loneliness. "Watch and pray so that you will not fall into temptation. The spirit is willing, but the body is weak" (Matthew 26:41 NIV).

YOU ARE NOT ALONE

If there is anything in this book that I want you to remember, it is the fact that *you are not alone*. You are not alone! Jesus says in John 10:27 that he knows us and we follow him. He goes on to say, "I give them [those who follow him] real and eternal life. They are protected from the Destroyer for good. No one can steal them from out of my hand. The Father who put them under my care is so much greater than the Destroyer and Thief" (verses 28–29).

Friend, the Destroyer wants to crush our marriages and our families, and one of the ways he does this is to convince you and me that we are by ourselves. That we have no one and there is no hope. He has used our country's recent wars to divide and conquer military families, and he often starts with the spouse. But we have promises from God to rely on and to remind us that he is with us. Here are a few:

> "The LORD is near to all who call on him, to all who call on him in truth" (Psalm 145:18 NIV).

> "My soul finds rest in God alone; my salvation comes from him. He alone is my rock and my salvation; he is my fortress, I will never be shaken" (Psalm 62:1–2 NIV).

> " 'Though the mountains be shaken and the hills be removed, yet my unfailing love for you will not be shaken nor my covenant of peace be removed,' says the LORD, who has compassion on you" (Isaiah 54:10 NIV).

> "Those who know your name will trust in you, for you, LORD, have never forsaken those who seek you" (Psalm 9:10 NIV).

> "GOD said, 'My presence will go with you. I'll see the journey to the end' " (Exodus 33:14).

We often believe that loneliness is not our choice. After all, it isn't our choice that our husbands deploy or that we're forced to move wherever the military tells us. But those are circumstances that leave us alone, not lonely. We choose whether we are lonely when we decide to reach out to others or stay to ourselves; when we stop being willing to connect with God and with other people or we find groups and activities we can be a part of; when we refuse to admit we need anyone, including God, or we are honest with ourselves and confess that we need help. That is when we choose, whether we realize it or not, if loneliness will be our friend.

One of the reasons I started Wives of Faith is because I did not want to fall into the trap of loneliness. I knew that while my husband was away, I needed other women around me whom I could talk to and pray with and be there for. We all have a desire to connect, and we all want to be understood. But it is so imperative that we first make sure our connection with God is strong, that we are looking up and staying focused on his plan and his truths for life before we look to others to fill those needs. He is our ultimate friend and comforter.

Let me say a word about friends, because this is an issue I have learned the hard way. Particularly for Guard and Reserve spouses who live in civilian communities with only civilian friends and no direct contact with other military wives, it can be easy to isolate ourselves, even from those friends we already have. When our circumstances change, as in the case of a deployment, life can appear to be quite out of the norm. So we try to order our lives in other ways, maybe convincing ourselves that now we really don't have anything in common with our friends. Their lives are continuing as they were; ours have changed significantly.

I have to confess that this happened to me; it was frustrating for me that my two closest friends (part of two couples my husband and I did a lot with) didn't seem to get what I was dealing with. They stopped calling regularly, and when they did call, it was usually because they needed a favor, not because they wanted to see how I was doing. They rarely asked about my husband, and their husbands sent very few emails to let him know they were thinking about him. I started resenting the fact that their situations were so different from my own, and gradually, I let the friendships end. In hindsight, I wish I had done things differently. Though I thought of these two friends as my closest friends and tried to explain how I was feeling and expected them to reciprocate, I should have accepted the friendships for what they were and not discounted them altogether.

The longer I work in women's ministry, the more I learn that just as there are many different personalities among women, there are also many different kinds of friendships. I have friends I love for their spiritual maturity and friends I appreciate for their zest for life. There are younger women who remind me it's okay to have a little fun sometimes, and there are older women who know how to offer wise counsel when I'm making hard decisions. There is something you can learn or receive from anyone who connects with your life, and they can learn and receive from you. You only have to have the patience to discover what that is.

Encourage Someone Else

The best way I've learned to overcome loneliness and to focus upward instead of inward is to find someone else to encourage. Studies have shown that taking the time to help someone else feel better often has the same result for you.

Reaching out can be easier for some than others. Most people would not think of me as an introvert because of what I do, but I am much more comfortable sitting in front of my computer at home than in a group meeting new people. But I realized quite a while ago that the joy I receive from talking with someone else and maybe helping put a smile on their face is far better than sitting at home in my comfort zone.

The benefit of mutual encouragement is one of the reasons we encourage ladies to connect in small groups through Wives of Faith and not just attend our bigger events. We want women to form friendships and to have the support they need to grow in their relationships. All it requires is a willingness to take the first step: ask your church to put a note in the bulletin or newsletter requesting that other military wives contact you. Or put a notice in your community paper. Or find friends on any of the social networking sites, blogs, and message boards out there today, and when you discover someone who lives close to you, set up a time to meet for coffee or for lunch! Email and phone calls can also be tools to encourage, but face to face is always best. There is something special about being able to see someone else's eyes and hear another's voice. We feel more grounded and less alone. And frankly, giggles and laughter are a whole lot better when they are shared with someone! Laughing in front of my computer monitor just isn't the same.

KNOW WHEN IT'S TIME TO ASK FOR HELP

Something very important to note: loneliness can be overcome by focusing more on God and less on yourself and by getting out and being active, finding ways to help others and to be an encourager. However, if you still feel heaviness, if the loneliness and sadness and hopeless feelings remain, if you struggle to sleep or find yourself wanting to sleep all the time, it's critical that you talk to someone — a doctor, a pastor, or a trusted counselor who can help you sort out what's going on. Depression is a serious condition that shouldn't be ignored, and it is treatable. Military OneSource is a great resource that you can contact for help, and as a military spouse, you are eligible for a referral to see a counselor in your area for up to twelve free visits per issue. For more information, visit www.militaryonesource.com.

Strength Builders

"For none of us lives to himself alone and none of us dies to himself alone" (Romans 14:7 NIV).

"I'll never forget the trouble, the utter lostness, the taste of ashes, the poison I've swallowed. I remember it all—oh, how well I remember—the feeling of hitting the bottom. But there's one other thing I remember, and remembering, I keep a grip on hope: God's loyal love couldn't have run out, his merciful love couldn't have dried up. They're created new every morning. How great your faithfulness! I'm sticking with God (I say it over and over). He's all I've got left" (Lamentations 3:19–24).

"God is a safe place to hide, ready to help when we need him" (Psalm 46:1).

"So speak encouraging words to one another. Build up hope so you'll all be together in this, no one left out, no one left behind" (1 Thessalonians 5:11).

"My soul finds rest in God alone" (Psalm 62:1 NIV).

Strength Trainers

1. In what ways do you find yourself struggling with loneliness?

2. How do you usually cope with being alone? How often do you turn to God to fill your loneliness?

3. How can you avoid getting sucked into self-pity? What are some of the things you can do to get the focus off yourself?

4. Is there someone you know who could use some encouragement this week? Write that person's name down and how and when you will be an encourager to them.

CHAPTER FIVE

SUPERWOMEN
GET GRACE TOO

★ ★ ★ ★ ★ ★

I MET TARA at our first regional event of the year for Wives of Faith. I had just finished speaking, and we were getting ready to go into some fun icebreakers when she came up to let me know she had to leave early to get back to her baby, who was sick.

"I just want you to know how much I appreciate what you said tonight, and that I'm glad I came," she said. She was young, and she looked very tired.

"Is everything okay?" I asked. Suddenly, her eyes filled with tears. I walked with her to the hall, where we could have some privacy, and she shared with me her story.

Tara's husband had deployed that very day for a four-month tour in Afghanistan with his Air Force unit. Two weeks earlier, she had left their home in North Carolina to live with her mother in Tennessee so she could get some support with their sons, an eighteen-month-old and a six-week-old. But her mother worked a full-time job and her baby was very sick with a respiratory syncytial virus (RSV) infection and had already been in the hospital once. The fear that her child might stop breathing in the middle of the night was keeping Tara from getting any sleep. And her older son was having a hard time with all of the changes — a new baby, a move, and his daddy's absence. Stress and distress had moved with Tara, and they didn't seem to be going away!

After we took some time to pray, I got her contact information and told her that our core group of ladies would try to find her some help, and that all of us would definitely be praying.

Since Tara was trying to squeeze in what little sleep she could when she could, phone calls weren't a great idea, and so the next day we started emailing. I contacted the church where we met to see if there might be any volunteers who would be willing to help. I thought if someone could just come over and sit a couple of hours, a few days a week, that would help Tara catch up on her sleep and feel more like a person and less of a zombie. Exhaustion doesn't just weaken the immune system; it can also heavily impact our perspective on what we're facing.

Many volunteers came forward, overwhelming Tara with the idea that so many strangers were willing to help her and her kids. But the best solution was found when the church decided they could send one of their paid childcare workers to Tara's house two days a week for the next month.

This was great news! I was so excited we had found a way to help this young military wife, but now it was up to Tara to accept the help. I tried putting myself in her shoes; as much as I would love the help, it would be hard to say yes. Military wives are supposed to be tough, and moms especially should be able to take care of everything and do everything for their children, right? Taking help would be a little like saying I *can't* do it all, wouldn't it?

Tara and I talked about this through email. "One piece of advice I've heard from other wives that I'll pass on to you," I wrote, "is don't try to be superwoman. Don't ask more of yourself than you would, say, a friend who is going through deployment. And make sure you get the rest you need. Take care of yourself; otherwise it will be harder to take care of your children."

Then Tara wrote back, "I had signed off and gone on to other things when I realized that I'm not sure how I can *not* try to be supermom. I understand what you are saying, but how do you do that when there are things that have to be done? Laundry has to be done, food cooked, babies fed, bills paid, house cleaned, babies gotten up with at night, diapers changed, cars fixed, all these things ... if there is no one else, then you have to do them, and like it or not, you have to be supermom. How can you not ask it of yourself when it is what is required?"

Tara's question may be one you've asked yourself during the course of a long week, in the middle of the night as you take care of a sick child, or in the early morning hours as you get lunches ready and backpacks checked before heading off to a full day of work yourself. Or if you haven't asked the question, "How can I not be superwoman?" you may have said the equivalent: "If I don't do it, it doesn't get done."

"If I don't do it, it doesn't get done." These are hard words, my friend, to live by. I know, because I've said them myself at various seasons of my life. The question Tara asked has a lot of truth to it, because we are often put in the position of being the only ones to take care of everything. We are responsible for our children, for our homes, for making sure that things get done, and life goes on with or without our husbands by our sides to help us. But how much of the weight of those things is self-inflicted?

I think it has a lot to do with perspective.

LOOK UP!

I know an author who is very particular about the angle that is used when she has her picture taken. She's a heavyset woman who had the misfortune one day of being set up for a photo shoot with a photographer who insisted on photographing her from the ground up while she stood, looking down. Well, ask any woman who is at all self-conscious about how she looks and she will tell you right away that this is the worst view you can use, because it shows every bump, lump, and double chin there is! But as my friend learned, if a camera is raised to a height higher than you and you are forced to look up into the lens, the extra weight disappears.

When we perceive that everything is up to us, that we are responsible for it all, and that success or failure rests completely on what we do, that's when our nose is to the grindstone. We hold on to the burdens and the stress and we struggle to have all the answers, especially when things don't go right — and there will be times things don't go right! We can find ourselves looking down constantly, and all of the weight of those worries and fears and stresses becomes evident, not just in our faces but in our spirits, not just in our physical being but in our emotions as well.

But when we look up, when we take the gaze off of ourselves and we focus on God, we can experience the grace he has for us. So the laundry doesn't get done in one day; maybe you have to say no to something or you just run out of time. God doesn't ask for perfection; he asks for obedience. He doesn't want our completed to-do lists. He just wants our hearts. When we look up, guess what he sees? Not the lumps or bumps or double chins. Instead, God sees his beautiful and trusting daughter looking to him for the answers and not trying to find them on her own.

If you think about it, we are born with the capacity to accept grace, which I define as free and unearned favor. A baby can't do anything on her own, or at least not very much. She is dependent on the grace of her parents to give her what she needs, and she is very much okay with that. You don't see a baby apologizing to her mother for being unable to fix her own bottle.

But somewhere between infancy and adulthood, we start thinking differently. We realize that setting the table can earn us an extra piece of chocolate cake for dessert. That making good grades keeps us out of the principal's office and puts us first in line for the class trip. We buy into the belief that by doing everything—and doing it perfectly—we magically earn the right to be in control or have more say in what happens in our lives.

Think about the mouse that runs through the maze. He isn't running because he wants to be the fastest mouse or break some mouse world record. He's running because he knows there is cheese at the end for his reward, and he knows if he runs fast enough, straight enough, smart enough, he will get that cheese. He will earn that cheese. But God doesn't insist on our jumping hurdles and running in mouse wheels. He gives us the cheese up front. No maze required.

THE ULTIMATE SUPERWOMAN

So it's easy to say and maybe even believe that God gives us grace and that we shouldn't try to be superwomen; it's

Survival Sisters
Dead Birds and Grace Too

The dead bird just about did me in.

It was the last straw. So to speak.

My chaplain husband had been absent from our home in the northern plains for four months already, and while he was not scheduled for a homebound flight, exactly, he was expecting to return home within two weeks. It was one of those "hurry up and wait" situations: be ready to leave at any time, but we don't have room for you yet on any transport flights.

Nevertheless, the end was in sight.

So was the dead robin outside my oldest daughter's window.

Everyone who knows me knows how squeamish I am. I have freaked out at any dead thing in my home, be it a mouse in a trap, a spider, or even dead flies. Eew.

So when we saw the dead bird outside her second-story window on the roof, which was also above our living room window, it was one of those "eew" moments.

I knew I couldn't leave the thing to rot. Not only was it unsanitary and unsightly, it was attracting a swarm of bees. I did not want those bees to buzz around her window. It was still open-window season.

The first question was, "Lord, why did this have to happen while my husband is away?"

When the heavens were silent, that brought me to my next question: how was I ever going to get that bird off the overhang so I could throw it away?

Pop the screen off the window, I thought. Then I could use a broom handle covered by a plastic bag to push it down so I could dispose of the carcass, and then pop the screen back in. Easy.

So I did.

Dead birdie, sans buzzing, living neck ornament (aka the bees), was carried off to the dumpster without delay!

All was okay until I couldn't get the screen back on. I tried and tried, smashing my fingertips and getting black screen ick all over my hands. Try as I might, I could not get that screen back in the window. I was so frustrated I began to cry!

In the process of removing the screen, I'd also broken my daughter's flimsy, yet icky, window shade. We were going to replace it anyway, but still! To break it when she had no screen was just bad icing on top of a really bad cake.

I wish I could sit here over a year later, now that the screen is fixed and the new shade installed (both by my husband after he came safely home), and tell you that I handled this whole incident well. Unfortunately, I cannot. I remember this day as the Great Meltdown of Deployment 2007. I had driven my girls all over the Midwest all summer, attended my twentieth high school reunion alone, dealt with a broken-down vehicle of my own *and* my mother's, handled everything myself as well as I could, and lost a friend to cancer. But I was done in by a dead bird.

I learned some things, though: life goes on whether our husbands are home or not. Something *will* break while he's away. (During his most recent TDY it was the garage door!) AAA is invaluable (even if only for the security of free towing and for fun stuff like free maps). Most important, however, I learned that God is always with me. He holds us all in his mighty hand.

Grace is unmerited favor, something I am given but do not deserve. God extended grace to me during that summer. He gave my minister husband a new mission, this exciting military ministry, beyond anything we ever imagined. He graciously granted me friends, who laughed and cried with me as I survived our first deployment. He gave me new mercies each morning, just as he promised in his Word. He is in control, and while his eye might be on the sparrow, it's also on the dead, bee-covered robin — and the separated family that lives where it died.

John 1:16: "From the fullness of his grace we have all received one blessing after another" (NIV).

— *Pattie Reitz,*
Air Force wife

a much harder thing to actually do and live out. Especially when we read about the woman in Proverbs 31:10–31. When I was a college student, the "Proverbs 31 woman," the wife whom the New International Version calls "of noble character" and *The Message* calls "a good wife," was just who I aspired to be. You may have had a similar aspiration. I wanted to be that woman who was the best wife; I wanted to be the mother who could do no wrong and do it all with precision and excellence.

But after I became a wife, and then a mother, and the hectic pace of life started accelerating, that idealistic goal dimmed. Martha Stewart, I quickly learned, I was not. And I no longer enjoyed reading about the Proverbs 31 woman, because I didn't believe there was any way I could ever be like her.

Let's look at the Proverbs 31 woman's story from a slightly different perspective.

THE PROVERBS 31 MILITARY WIFE

(Proverbs 31:10–31, paraphrasing *The Message*)

A good military wife is hard to find, and worth far more than medals of honor.

Her husband trusts her with everything and never has reason to regret it; he doesn't ever question her about any of the decisions she makes for their home or for their children.

Never spiteful or resentful when he leaves with little to no notice for months or for more than a year at a time, she treats him generously all her life long, waving goodbye with a smile and welcoming him home with a warm embrace, leaving the honey-do list in a drawer.

She can hunt for bargains and clip coupons with ease, and some of her happiest moments are the hours she spends in yard sales and thrift stores finding incredible deals on like-new clothing for her family. Her creativity in finding the perfect items for her care packages can't be matched, and her husband always mentions it.

She's like a retail buyer who travels to fun, faraway places and brings back exotic and interesting surprises.

She's always up before dawn, preparing breakfast for her family and organizing her day, keeping her kids on-task and her husband informed. A date is never forgotten, a social obligation never missed.

She can pack up and move her entire household by herself with no problems. And the money she saves in the selling and purchasing of her home because of her sharp skills in negotiation she shrewdly invests, doubling and tripling her family's income.

First thing in the morning, she dresses for work, rolls up her sleeves, and is eager to get started. She never has a bad day.

She always knows how important her role is and how much others are grateful for her; she's never in a hurry to fall into bed and doesn't mind staying up late, finishing chores while the rest of her family sleeps.

She's skilled in the crafts of home and hearth, and she loves to do housework. She enjoys making gourmet meals every night that even her children love, and her house is always spotless. She lovingly sews her husband's rank patches or collar insignias on, no matter how late at night it is. She doesn't mind that he's had them for weeks but has told her only just now that he needs them for tomorrow morning.

She's quick to assist anyone in need, and gives many hours to the FRG and spouse club whenever help is needed. She greets each military wife she hears from with a smile, no matter what their complaint is.

She doesn't worry about her family when a change of orders comes; she homeschools her children so they are never behind in their education.

She makes her own clothing and always looks like she could be on the cover of a magazine, with or without makeup.

Her husband is greatly respected among his troops and has received many honors and promotions.

For extra money, she runs a successful direct-sales business, keeping her clients no matter how many moves she makes.

She is always confident and sure of herself; she faces tomorrow with a smile.

When she speaks she has something worthwhile to say, and she always says it kindly. She is never in a bad mood.

She keeps an eye on everyone in her household and keeps them all busy and productive, running them to practices and cheering them on at their sporting events, being both mother and father when needed.

Her children respect and love her; her husband is always telling her, "Many military wives have done wonderful things, but you've outclassed them all!"

But charm can mislead and beauty soon fades. The military wife to be admired and praised is the woman who lives in awe of God. Give her everything she deserves! (A day at the spa is a good start!)

Now, I've obviously written this a little in jest, poking fun at our perceptions of the perfect military wife. But how often do we see some of these qualities in other wives and wonder where they are in us? And how much more time do we spend trying to emulate these supposed ideals instead of focusing on the ideals God has for us as individuals?

FEAR THE LORD

If there is one verse that I want you to notice in the Proverbs 31 passage (the original text, not my paraphrase), it is not the verses about making homemade clothes or excelling at business. It's the second half of verse 30 — "but a woman who fears the LORD is to be praised" (NIV).

It's interesting that almost every verse in the Bible that mentions the word *fear*, if it's not saying "fear not," is talking about fearing God. Deuteronomy 6:13 says, "Fear the LORD your God, serve him only and take your oaths in his name" (NIV). Second Samuel 23:3 – 4 says, "When he rules in the fear of God, he is like the light of morning at sunrise" (NIV). Psalm 111:10 says, "The fear of the LORD is the beginning of wisdom" (NIV).

You can almost miss this part in Proverbs 31 about the woman who "fears the Lord" because it's tucked away after so much of the description of what the woman *does*, but this phrase describes how the woman *is*. We get so caught up in the *what* that we miss how we're supposed to *be*. She fears the Lord. This phrase is a description of her heart, her countenance, and her soul — her view from within that looks up to God and away from herself.

And in this instance, fear doesn't mean she is scared of God, running from him the way Adam and Eve did when they hid from him in the Garden after they sinned. No, in this situation, she is in *awe* of God, she walks in reverence and admiration and amazement of who God is and who he is in her life and what he means to her. And what she is in awe of most, we can presume, is the grace that God gives.

I mentioned this verse at the beginning of the book, but let's take another look at it. In Matthew 11, Jesus has been talking to a crowd that has gathered. He says, "Are you tired? Worn out? Burned out on religion? Come to me. Get away with me and you'll recover your life. I'll show you how to take a real rest. Walk with me and work with me — watch how I do it. *Learn the unforced rhythms of grace.* I won't lay anything heavy or ill-fitting on you. Keep company with me and you'll learn to live freely and lightly" (Matthew 11:28–30, emphasis mine).

"Unforced rhythms of grace." Doesn't that phrase sound wonderful? Don't you wish you could have that? I do. What does that look like? Rest for the weary. Light for the soul. Trying without struggling. Moving without sighing. I can have confidence in the knowledge that God is my strength. There is little stress. Little angst. A whole lot of hope.

We are the ones who bring "heavy" or "ill-fitting" stress-filled clutter into our lives when we say yes instead of no, or jump into things we think we should do instead of praying about it first, or add stress and worry to our load of responsibilities. But just as Jesus told Martha, we must remember, "You're fussing far too much and getting yourself worked up over nothing. One thing only is essential, and Mary has chosen it" (Luke 10:41–42).

That one thing Mary chose was to keep her eyes on Jesus. This is also the answer he gives to us. "Come to me. Get away with me and you'll recover your life. I'll show you how to take a real rest. Walk with me and work with me — watch how I do it."

Let's pause for a moment on that idea. I once heard a popular woman evangelist talk about how Jesus is the only thing we need. "Just give me Jesus," she said, over and over again. I must admit that at the time, her words grated against something inside of me. I'm not sure why; I knew the point she was trying to make. In my head, in my heart, I knew that Jesus *is* everything we need.

But I couldn't help picturing how those words might sound to a military wife in her ninth month of a deployment who has a car that keeps breaking down and a child who is throwing up, a wife who hasn't gotten a good night's sleep since her husband left and who spends what time she does get by herself in her bathtub with the tears rolling down her face. Easy to say those words in a church service with hearty "amens" all around; much harder to whisper them in the chaos all around you. If you said those words, would you believe them? And if you believed them, would you trust that they are true? Can you say those words today?

The Gift of Grace

God does not want our perfect works; he simply wants our hearts. None of our efforts can impress God, because he already loves us, so who are we really doing everything for? Why do we get ourselves in knots trying to do everything, to *be* everything, like a superwoman often does? Who called us to be superwomen? Who asked us to be super military wives?

Not God.

The world says, "Be more than what you are," but God says, "Just be. Be in my presence. Be in my love. Be in my grace. You're fussing far too much. You're getting worked up over nothing."

He has given us something better. A gift that is bigger than a clean house and better than a care package just for you. He's given us a gift that lasts, and it's his ultimate gift of grace for us.

And it's Jesus. He is our gift.

Look at what Jesus says in John 16:23–24: "This is what I want you to do: Ask the Father for whatever is in keeping with the things I've revealed to you. Ask in my name, according to my will, and he'll most certainly give it to you. Your joy will be a river overflowing its banks!"

Jesus *is* all we need, because it is through him that our needs are met. He tells us in Matthew 6:31–33 that what he's trying to do for you is "to get you to relax, to not be so preoccupied with *getting*, so you can respond to God's *giving*. People who don't know God and the way he works fuss over these things, but you know both God and how he works. Steep your life in God-reality, God-initiative, God-provisions. Don't worry about missing out. You'll find all your everyday human concerns will be met."

So when the sink backs up or the to-do list is two pages long and counting, what if instead of stressing out and getting upset we stopped for a moment and prayed? What if we asked ourselves, "What would Jesus do?" before we made our plans for the day. Would it eliminate some distractions? Would it focus us on what's most important? Would we become more God Strong and less Me Strong?

"For by grace are you saved through faith, and not by your own efforts. It's a gift from God" (Ephesians 2:8, my paraphrase). If I were to give you something of great value, a beautiful diamond necklace that's worth eighty thousand dollars, and tell you that I'll give it to you for just a hundred dollars, you might say, "I thought you were going to give it to me." Because even though it's a great price, the necklace isn't a gift if you have to pay for it. You receive it because you've paid for it. So if I am saved through God's grace plus anything else—my time, my hard work, my efforts—then the grace is no longer grace. It's canceled out.

Grace is a gift; there are no requirements or fine print. Nothing we can do can persuade God to show favor to us. This treasure comes strictly from him. A gift that is free, bringing the freedom we long for.

A soldier once told me about a conversation he had with an Iraqi translator he was traveling with one day just outside of Baghdad. The Iraqi was trying to understand the meaning of the English word *freedom*. After several unsuccessful attempts, the soldier finally pointed out a bird that was flying just above them. The Iraqi turned and smiled at the soldier and waved his arms slowly, his head nodding excitedly. "Freedom!"

As military wives, we do not have to be chained to the expectations of others and of ourselves when we have the freedom that only God's grace can give us. The Proverbs 31 woman had freedom to do all of those things she did and to do them well because she kept God in the center of her life. That doesn't mean we will be able to do all of those things, but we should feel a freedom in our spirits and in our lives when we make the time to stand in awe of him and are receptive to his grace and the gift he gives us, the freedom we have in Christ.

As a military wife, it is my natural tendency to *do*. But God is asking me to learn to *be*. And through his grace, I can.

STRENGTH BUILDERS

"Let me put this question to you: How did your new life begin? Was it by working your heads off to please God? Or was it by responding to God's Message to you? Are you going to continue this craziness? For only crazy people would think they could complete by their own efforts what was begun by God. If you weren't smart enough or strong enough to begin it, how do you suppose you could perfect it? Did you go through this whole painful learning process for nothing? It is not yet a total loss, but it certainly will be if you keep this up!" (Galatians 3:2–4).

"My grace is enough; it's all you need. My strength comes into its own in your weakness" (2 Corinthians 12:9).

"What I'm trying to do here is to get you to relax, to not be so preoccupied with *getting* so you can respond to God's *giving*. People who don't know God and the way he works fuss over these things, but you know both God and how he works" (Matthew 6:31–33).

"And don't take yourself too seriously—take God seriously" (Micah 6:8).

"They found grace out in the desert, these people who survived the killing. Israel, out looking for a place to rest, met God out looking for them!" (Jeremiah 31:2).

STRENGTH TRAINERS

1. How often do you rely on God's grace in your life? When are you most likely to forget?

2. What are some ways you can reduce your quest to be superwoman? What are some things you need to say no to?

3. What are things you catch yourself doing in order to emulate the Proverbs 31 military wife? What, of those, can you make less important?

4. Describe what it means to fear the Lord. What are some ways that we can do that?

5. What has Jesus done for you through the gift of his grace? Start a list and keep it where you can look at it often.

CHAPTER SIX

GOD IS IN CONTROL

★ ★ ★ ★ ★

LATE ONE NIGHT my cell phone rang. In the dark, I reached over to my nightstand and picked it up. An unfamiliar area code and number lit up the screen, and I smiled, 99 percent sure it was my husband. Cliff had been in Iraq for a little over a month, and he had finally settled into something of a schedule. We were able to talk a few times a week, either by phone or computer. Normally, he tried calling me while he was winding down after his twelve-hour workday and I was just getting up to start mine. But I didn't mind the wake-up. I was happy just being able to hear his voice.

I sleepily said, "Hello?"

There was a brief delay and then I heard his voice. "Hey, you. Sorry if I woke you."

I looked at the clock. It wasn't quite midnight. "Oh, that's okay, honey. I'm just glad you called. How is everything going?"

My eyes half closed, I listened as he told me a little bit about his day, or rather night. Since it had gotten hotter, they were working through the night when it was only ninety degrees instead of the daytime temps of 120 in the shade. Working with Special Forces, there wasn't a whole lot he could say, but he told me what he could. That he'd gotten the care package I had sent him, and he was putting a letter for me in the mail soon. That it had been very busy, and he was tired.

"I think the guys and I are going to go grab some dinner at Taco Bell," he said.

I sat up and my heart started beating faster. I looked through the dark in the direction of the picture of us on our wedding day. Before he deployed, we had chosen "Taco Bell" as the code word that he would use if he ever had to leave the base. In military lingo, if he ever had to travel "outside the wire." If he ever had to travel to dangerous parts unknown.

I tried not to sound panicky. "What?"

In my mind, I knew this would happen, but since he'd arrived in Iraq, my heart had convinced me it wouldn't. After all, it sounded to me like he was staying plenty busy on the base; I was sure he would stay there the entire deployment.

I have never felt more helpless than I did at that moment. What could I say? What could I do?

There was absolutely nothing I could do. As much as I wanted to reach my arms through the phone and pull him close and keep him with me, his mission, and his life, were out of my hands.

"I'll be okay," he said, picking up on my emotions through the silence he was hearing on the other end. "And I'll call you as soon as I can. I gotta get off soon. Do you want to pray real quick?"

"Yes," I said, trying to stifle a sob.

As Cliff softly prayed, I thought about how much I love this man, his smile, his easygoing manner, his wonderful relationship with our son. I knew nothing about the mission he was about to go on—if it would be safe, if it would be risky. Then it was my turn to pray.

"God, please be with Cliff over the next few days and keep him safe." As I prayed, just above a whisper, my voice cracked. My words said *please* but my tone and my heart were saying much more, almost demanding, "God, you *will* keep my husband safe and you *will* bring him back to me!"

After Cliff and I hung up, I lay back down and let the tears fall. I felt guilty for how I had just talked to God. I knew that he is in charge, that I'm not. I knew that he is in control of my husband's life "over there" just as he is when Cliff is home with me. Nothing about that had changed. What had changed was my trust. What had changed was my certainty that God really does want the best for my family. I suddenly began to doubt. Was it possible that God would let Cliff get hurt? Or killed?

That night, I felt God clearly speaking to me. In my heart, I heard him say, *Sara, do you trust me?*

"Yes, God, I do. At least I'm trying to."

Do you believe I'm in control?

"Yes."

Then trust me. And know that I'm taking care of Cliff just as I am taking care of you and Caleb. And that whatever happens, I know the plans I have for you.

That night, I learned what it means to leave my burdens at the feet of Jesus. And that if the worst were to happen—whether my husband were to die in combat or in a car accident while at home—God is still in control. And he would walk with me through the hurts and the pain. He would be strong for me in my weakness, and he would give me enough of his grace and love to keep going.

That part would never change.

LIVING OUT
WHAT WE BELIEVE

What did have to change was my attitude, my behavior, and my actions. If I really believe that God is in control, then my life needs to reflect that, right?

God *is* in control. We know this because the Bible says so. In Ephesians 2, we're told that we "neither make nor save ourselves. God does both the making and saving" (Ephesians 2:8). But though we know this truth, it's sometimes harder to truly believe it and then live it out.

I think it's easier to believe God is in control when tragedy has already struck and we have no way of understanding why. Take, for example, the hundreds of thousands of people who flocked to churches and synagogues in the days after terrorists attacked our country on September 11, 2001. There was no understanding that day, and so we looked to God. We did not know when the next attack might occur; we did not know how our husbands would be affected in their service to our country, or when those husbands who left almost immediately after the attacks would return. The unknown loomed large before us, so we were very willing to say, "God is in control; God is with us." We were unable to grasp or see into the unkown, so we collectively held our breath and hoped that God could see and know more than we knew ourselves.

But time passed, and as a nation, despite being in two wars, despite having our neighbors and our brothers and our sisters and our spouses leave for untold amounts of time, we started feeling safer. Bad things didn't happen. Life got back to "normal." We got used to taking our shoes off at the airport and leaving our nail clippers at home. The worry and fear subsided a little. The threat wasn't so immediate anymore. At least it felt that way. And God once again went from being with us and in control to being "out there." Somewhere. The remote control was in our hands once again, and we wanted to make sure that the channel we were watching was something we really wanted to see.

Or what about the trouble we have seen with our economy in recent years? I think this one can be more difficult for us when it comes to leaning on God for strength and trusting he is in control. A job loss is not a plane flying into a tower, but for the person who has lost the job, it can feel that way. When a struggling economy forces higher prices on an already tight budget, we can panic and wonder what steps we can take to turn this sinking ship around!

As a type-A personality, I definitely struggle between wanting to be in control and stepping back and remembering that God is in control. Of course, military wives are used to not always being in control. The military is notorious for changing orders, delaying assignments, throwing kinks into schedules and plans, and complicating permanent change of station (PCS) moves. But most of us would admit that we still like to have as much control as possible. That probably explains why some wives keep five or six different types of window treatments under their beds so they will always be ready for the next set of windows they encounter.

But the question for us is not whether God is in control; most of us, if we already have a relationship with him, understand that he is. The question we are faced with is, Are we following God, or are we trying to lead instead?

Letting God
Be the Pace Car

My husband and I have enjoyed helping in the children's ministry at our church on Sunday nights. Melissa, one of the ministry assistants for the children's area, is a huge NASCAR fan. She loves to watch the races, and on Sunday afternoons, when we have to spend hours listening to kids audition for a church musical, you can bet that she will have her laptop out, quietly monitoring the races and how her beloved Jeff Gordon is doing.

One of the important elements of a NASCAR race that I've learned about recently is the pace car. A pace car is the safety car, because when it is out on the track, the rest of the cars are required to stay behind it. This car sets the speed, or the pace, of the pack, usually slowing the cars down during a caution period after a major accident or when there is too much debris on the track. When the pace car is out, it's easier for the other cars to make pit stops, and when they are on the track behind the pace car, they use less fuel and can drive longer on one tank of gas. Because of the pace car, they can often make one less stop, saving time and improving their chances of winning.

What would happen if we allowed God to be our pace car for life, setting the speed, slowing us down when we need to be slowed, and warning us when there is debris or trouble ahead? Would we have fewer accidents? More successful laps? Easier turns? Faster times? More fuel for the finish line?

WHAT IT MEANS
TO FOLLOW GOD

In order to follow God and his timing for my life, my will has to come after his. My directions must come from him. This isn't easy for me, because I think I have some really good ideas on what I should be doing and where my life should go! But what I want and what God wants are often two very different things, and his way is always better.

Think of the caterpillar, who sits in his cocoon waiting to become a beautiful butterfly. If God's plan for that caterpillar is followed and he exits the cocoon when he is supposed to, the fluid in his body will be squeezed out into his wings, and he will be ready to fly. But if someone comes along and tries to speed up that process by opening the cocoon, that important fluid will never be pushed out where it needs to go. His wings will be so tiny and weak compared with his large body, he will be unable to fly and he will die. In the same way, if we try to rush ahead of God, we may miss some important lessons we need to learn in order to be able to handle the responsibilities and tasks he has planned for us.

For most of my childhood and on into college, I thought I was supposed to be a singer. I loved music and I loved singing, so I was positive that music was where God wanted to use me. In college, I majored in music, sang in music groups, and tried my hand at songwriting and composing. But by my sophomore year, I had burned out on studying classical music and decided to take a break from school, coming home to work in Christian radio and plan my wedding. In a span of six months after my husband and I got married in

1998, God used two moments to make very clear to me what he wanted for my life. Or more accurate, what he didn't do.

The first was an invitation by a pastor of a small church in my hometown to serve as the music director. I was overjoyed! My dream since I had started college was to serve as a minister for a church somewhere. I had learned very quickly, however, that there were still many barriers for women in my denomination, and unless I was content to work with only the children, there would not be a lot of opportunities for me to serve as a music minister. So this invitation from the pastor was nothing short of a miracle, and I just knew this was something only God could have provided.

But I didn't expect what happened next. The more I prayed about the opportunity, the more I felt I wasn't supposed to take the position. This was confusing for me, because for many years, I had felt this was God's plan. But instead of feeling joy and excitement and exhilaration, I was feeling stress and uncertainty and tension. With this offer, which I had looked forward to for so long, now right in front of me, I should have felt incredible peace. But instead I felt the opposite.

My husband supported my decision to turn down the church's invitation to serve, and we soon set out on a different course, moving away from our friends and family to Tennessee, where we both worked to finish our degrees at Union University. I continued studying for my music degree, but my passion was growing for communications. As a way to help pay the bills, I applied to be a student worker in the university's office of university relations. Less than a month after I started, my boss, the news director, resigned, and while the university looked for a replacement, I began filling in as I could.

That's when the next moment happened. A new voice studio opened in the area, and I was invited to take a job there as a voice teacher. *Surely,* I thought, *this is what I'm supposed to do. After all, I am specializing in voice!* But the more I prayed about it, the more I felt it wasn't the direction God wanted me to go.

Now I was seeking God in great earnest. What *was* his plan for me? What did he want from me? What was I supposed to do?

Two days later, I sat down with my husband. "Um, I feel really silly saying this, but I think God wants me to apply for the news director job." I mean, this was crazy talk. What college or university would hire a staff member who didn't have a college degree?

But the feeling didn't go away, and the next day I went in and talked with my supervisor. Three days later I was hired.

I share this story with you only because I want you to see that following God often means taking risks and getting out of our comfort zones and letting go of preconceived notions. Looking back, I know that following God's leading at that time in my life was a critical point for me. Taking that step of faith and trusting that God is in control instead of trying to run ahead of him opened doors and sent me on a journey I never could have planned for myself.

This doesn't mean my journey has been completed or that I always and correctly follow God's direction. For as many times as I've followed him and seen him work in my life, I'm sad to say there also have been times I've gone off and done my own thing, veering off-course and usually with very messy or disappointing results. Shortly after taking a position as a corporate staff writer for a large Christian publisher—a role I felt God had opened the door for me to have—I grew discontented with being "just" a writer. I wanted to do more with media, as I had done in my previous job as a university news director, and gradually convinced my boss to make it so. But almost as soon as my title changed, so did my heart, and I realized that what I had wanted was not necessarily what God wanted. I was constantly swimming upstream, and by the time I left that job to work from home, I had experienced a lot of heartache and stress.

THE GOD STRONG ZONE

Following God and accepting his control in my life requires more than just an awareness of what he wants to do. Following God means being obedient, and that is a very hard word for us to hear sometimes. Our husbands are perhaps a little more used to this word than we are; when they are given orders, they're expected to obey them. But God also expects us to follow his commands, his teachings, and his instructions.

Doing this doesn't come without its share of fear. Just yesterday, I talked with a Reserve wife who has recently felt a very clear tug on her heart from God to start serving other military wives and to do that through Wives of Faith. She admitted that it was a very scary idea to think about! She had seeds of doubt: she wasn't a good enough writer; she has never experienced active military life, so how could she serve active wives? But God is calling her to something bigger than herself. She is being stretched beyond her comfort zone, and because of that, she is being forced to stay

Survival Sisters
God's Assignment

"We're getting an assignment." These words always catch me a little off-guard. You would think that nineteen years of Air Force life would teach me not to be surprised by these four words, but they always seem to evoke such mixed emotions: excitement and fear, relief and concern, woo-hoo! and oh no! all at the same time. Our assignments used to run three to four years, but now they seem to come every two years or less, depending on school opportunities, career progression, and other reasons. I always welcomed these changes as a chance to learn new things and see new places.

But three kids later, new assignments usually bring thoughts like, *What are the schools like? How will the kids feel about making new friends? How do I feel about looking for a new job? How often will my husband be home for us?* It seems like the world sort of closes in on me as I ready the packing, examine housing opportunities, research schools, and prepare to restart our lives once again.

Recently one of our pastors at church spoke about getting bogged down in our circumstances. He explained that we get hung up in the "why me" as opposed to looking for the opportunity that God is placing before us. He said we should realize that *this* life and *these* circumstances are not by chance; they are our assignments from God. "*This* is the life that I have been assigned by God? It's my assignment?" Now that is a thought I can wrap my head around! Finally, things started making sense to me. God has brought us here to do something!

I could not have imagined God's plan when my husband announced that we were moving to Grand Forks, North Dakota.

Check your maps; this is no place for a southern gal like me, since it is right on the Canadian border. My husband giggled when he shared the news. "Honey, *you* said we joined the Air Force to see new places, so I told my boss that this was going to be great!"

Really, I could have choked him for being so excited. There are no big airports, lots of open empty space, and yes, the temps reach negative forty in the winter. What was God's assignment? To find a church and learn how to be more active in our faith? No doubt there. To learn how to handle major changes in my husband's career? He was declared a diabetic, lost flying status, took a significant pay cut, and lost an opportunity to command a squadron. We weren't even sure he was going to be allowed to remain on active duty. I got very depressed, but God was faithful and blessed me with friends who had insight. Friends who told me that I needed to see opportunity instead of roadblocks. Why? Because that roadblock is what brought us to Nashville, my hometown.

This assignment has given us a wonderful church home, where my oldest came to really know God. This assignment (from God) has brought me a job that I love. This assignment (from God and the Air Force) has blessed us with a squadron where we (as a team) can have real impact in lives that have been longing for care. Our squadron covers eight states, and none of us is anywhere near a base. We have spouse meetings via the internet … bizarre. This assignment to Nashville has brought me to Wives of Faith. This assignment has taught me that our lives reach beyond just what the Air Force has for us.

So what have I learned so far? I know that each assignment gives me the opportunity to do things a little better, to not repeat the mistakes of the past, to touch someone's life, to make a difference, and to be a positive reflection of God's love. I have the opportunity to be stronger, to be more faithful, and to handle whatever this world can throw at me because God has a special place for us.

Hey, guess what? Today presents a new assignment for you as well. What will you do with it?

— *Leanne Keirstead,*
Air Force wife

in the God Strong Zone, a place where we are constantly aware of our dependence on God.

In order to live in the God Strong Zone, we must be constantly mindful of God's presence in our lives, and we do that by reading his Word. I have noticed that when I consistently start my mornings with reading and some time in prayer, my days are not as hectic or don't feel as stressful as when I go for some time without reading and praying.

I experience the same feeling when I'm driving without my GPS and I'm trying to find a location I am not familiar with. I'm trying to look at street signs, read the scrawled notes in my hand, and avoid hitting other cars in the process! But when I have that calm and pleasant voice beside me telling me where I need to turn next and when I will arrive at my destination, I am a little more confident and much more relaxed. When I start my day off spending time with God, I am putting to good use my own spiritual GPS — God's Provision and Support!

A PSALM FOR THE DAY

Glenda, an Army Reserve wife, has also seen her GPS in action. Since 9/11, her husband, Charles, has been gone more than he has been home and at the time of this writing is currently serving his second tour in Iraq. One Tuesday morning, Glenda was feeling overwhelmed and decided to call her pastor for advice. She admitted that she normally didn't read her Bible during the week, and would like to but wasn't really sure where to start. One suggestion her pastor gave her was to read the psalm of the day; for instance, if it was the fiftieth day of the year, Psalm 50 would be her daily reading.

After not hearing from her husband for several days, Glenda grew increasingly worried. Between brief bouts of crying for her husband and checking her email to see if there was a message from him, Glenda forced herself to sit down and read the psalm for the day, Psalm 27.

> The LORD is my light and my salvation—
>   whom shall I fear?
> The LORD is the stronghold of my life—
>   of whom shall I be afraid?
> When evil men advance against me
>   to devour my flesh,
> when my enemies and my foes attack me,
>   they will stumble and fall.
> Though an army besiege me,
>   my heart will not fear;
> though war break out against me,
>   even then will I be confident.
>
> One thing I ask of the LORD,
>   this is what I seek:
> that I may dwell in the house of the LORD
>   all the days of my life,
> to gaze upon the beauty of the LORD
>   and to seek him in his temple.
> For in the day of trouble
>   he will keep me safe in his dwelling;
> he will hide me in the shelter of his tabernacle
>   and set me high upon a rock.
> Then my head will be exalted
>   above the enemies who surround me;
> at his tabernacle will I sacrifice with shouts of joy;
>   I will sing and make music to the LORD.

Hear my voice when I call, O LORD;
    be merciful to me and answer me.
My heart says of you, "Seek his face!"
    Your face, LORD, I will seek.
Do not hide your face from me,
    do not turn your servant away in anger;
    you have been my helper.
Do not reject me or forsake me,
    O God my Savior.
Though my father and mother forsake me,
    the LORD will receive me.
Teach me your way, O LORD;
    lead me in a straight path
    because of my oppressors.
Do not turn me over to the desire of my foes,
    for false witnesses rise up against me,
    breathing out violence.

I am still confident of this:
    I will see the goodness of the LORD
    in the land of the living.
Wait for the LORD;
    be strong and take heart
    and wait for the LORD.

—NIV

After reading that passage twice, in tears, actually praying the words for her husband, Glenda felt an incredible peace wash over her. For the rest of the day, she felt strong; she knew God was with her. What she didn't know at the time was that roughly an hour and a half after she read that passage, her husband and another soldier were on a mission when their Humvee hit an IED. Thankfully, both her husband and the driver survived, and though his back was hurt due to the force of the blast, Charles was expected to be okay.

In an email she shared with her friends and family, Glenda wrote, "Isn't God amazing? He had a plan. He prompted me to have that meltdown the week before and to call my pastor so I would have that passage for that specific day!"

Like the psalm reminded her, Glenda knew that God was keeping her and her husband "safe in his dwelling" and that she could "be strong and take heart" as she waited on God. Could Glenda have had a different response to her husband's injury had she not read that psalm that morning? Most likely, yes. But because she had been in God's Word, because God had met her where she was and had comforted her with the words she needed to hear that very moment, Glenda was able to see that God is in control, in good times and bad.

Let's take another look at the last verse in Psalm 27. "Wait for the LORD; be strong and take heart and wait for the LORD" (verse 14). *The Message* version reads, "Stay with GOD! Take heart. Don't quit. I'll say it again: Stay with GOD."

God is saying to you today, "Wait. Stay. Don't run ahead. Don't trail behind. Just stay with me. Give your worries to me. Give your fears to me. But also give me your plans. Give me your dreams. And let me turn those plans and those dreams into something better."

You may remember the story of Heather Mercer and Dayna Curry, the two relief workers who were imprisoned by the Taliban in Afghanistan shortly before US forces invaded

Kabul and rescued them in November of 2001. In a chapel service for the university where I once worked, the young women shared the story of their experience. Heather told how she had ended a serious relationship with her boyfriend because she had felt so strongly that God was calling her to go to Afghanistan. She was facing a choice between a good life and God's choice of the best life for her. She encouraged Christians not to settle for taking just God's good but to lose everything of themselves to take God's best.

When we acknowledge God's control in our lives, we forgo our good for his best. We trade fast food for fine dining. We give up the nice so we can have the incredible. We may not feel like we are trading up at first; to follow God's will often is counter to what society and culture says we should do. But over time, we discover the joy and the beauty and the riches of trusting in God's control, walking in his strength and his certainty. We learn firsthand what Romans 3:28 says, that "God does not respond to what *we* do; we respond to what *God* does. We've finally figured it out. Our lives get in step with God and all others by letting him set the pace, not by proudly or anxiously trying to run the parade."

How can you experience more of God's control in your life? Are there things in your life you need to let go of and give back to God? Your husband? Your marriage? Your children? Your ambitions and desires?

If you need to, take a sheet of paper and write your list down. Pray over these things and ask God to help you release them. He will.

STRENGTH BUILDERS

"We don't make God; he makes us, and all of this—sky, earth, sea, and everything in them" (Acts 14:15).

"I am GOD, the only God there is, the one and only. I promise in my own name: Every word out of my mouth does what it says. I never take back what I say" (Isaiah 45:23).

"Can the no-gods of the godless nations cause rain? Can the sky water the earth by itself? You're the one, O GOD, who does this. So you're the one for whom we wait. You made it all, you do it all" (Jeremiah 14:22).

"Then Jesus went to work on his disciples. 'Anyone who intends to come with me has to let me lead. You're not in the driver's seat; *I* am'" (Matthew 16:24).

"By entering through faith into what God has always wanted to do for us—set us right with him, make us fit for him—we have it all together with God because of our Master Jesus" (Romans 5:1).

STRENGTH TRAINERS

1. What are some of the areas of your life you try to control? How is that working for you?

2. What do you think your life would look like if you turned everything over to God? Could it be better than it is right now?

3. What will you need to do to experience the God Strong Zone in your life? What things will you need to lay down? What will you need to pick up?

4. Is God calling you to do something great over something that's just good? What is it? What is keeping you from answering that call? Take some time to pray and ask God to give you the courage to enter into the great plan he has for your life.

CHAPTER SEVEN

GOD KNOWS
MY HURTS

* * * * *

SOMETIMES WE MILITARY WIVES go out of our way *not* to share our hurts, as Angela did when her Navy Reserve husband was deployed. Knowing that her husband was in a dangerous area and worried about keeping his men alive, Angela made it a point when her husband called home never to talk about the tough things she was going through. Her tone was always upbeat, her stories always positive. She was protecting her husband and, in a sense, protecting his mission and ensuring he could keep his attention where it needed to be. Still, it made things harder for her when her husband came home; he couldn't understand that she too had experienced difficulty and stress and sorrow while he was away.

Whether or not you talk to your husband a great deal about what hurts you and what you wrestle with — and I hope that you have the type of relationship in which you can — all of us struggle with hurt and disappointment, and it's important to remember that God knows and understands. If we're not careful, we can convince ourselves that God doesn't realize when we hurt or that maybe he is happy when we're sad. But that isn't the case at all.

Life Isn't Perfect

I recently got an email from a Guard couple in our Sunday school class who were passing on a prayer request. A friend had previously been diagnosed with colon cancer, gone through surgery, and was in remission. He had resumed his normal activities and moved on with his life and his family, leaving the cancer experience behind him. Or so he thought.

One day he felt pain in his legs. After a visit to the doctor, he discovered that the cancer had spread to every part of his body. Just forty-one years old, this husband and father of a nine-year-old son was told he has only four weeks to live. Though he's made peace with what is happening and he's a strong believer and is trusting God no matter the outcome, he's worried about his son. He's taking his son to their pastor to sit down and talk, because he wants to make sure his son doesn't grow up blaming God for what happened to his dad.

Talk about a hurtful situation! I don't even know this family, and their story brought me to tears. You may know of stories like this one or you may have experienced hurts as painful as this in your own life. We don't like to hear things like this because they remind us just how vulnerable all of us are. Life isn't perfect—it isn't in the military and it isn't as a Christian.

I think we can make the mistake of seeing both the military and Christianity as answers to all of our problems. After all, many join the military because they hope, some-how, their lives will be better for it. When I was reporting on board the USS *Truman* in 2003 during the first week of the Iraq war, I slept in the female supply berthing area; it was a huge space underneath the flight deck with more than three hundred beds stacked three high. My rack was on the very top, and each time a jet took off or landed, the bed shook with the force of it.

On the *Truman* I met many of the women who called those tight quarters their home. They were young—nineteen, twenty, twenty-one years old—and as a mom of a little boy myself, it touched me to see the pictures hanging by their beds or resting on their pillows—photos of their babies and children who were back home with friends or grandparents. Many of them shared similar stories; they were single moms who had joined the Navy with hopes of going to college one day and making a better life for themselves and their kids. Some of them saw the Navy as their only choice.

I also met enlisted sailors who shared over lunch in the mess deck that they'd joined the Navy to learn discipline or a skill or to get out of a tough home situation. A lot of hopes and dreams rode on their decision to enlist.

Many couples join the military for economic reasons—educational benefits as well as a guaranteed income. What they often don't plan on is the likelihood of deployments and times apart.

If we're not careful, we can also approach the Christian life with those same hopes and dreams. We "enlist" in the Christian community thinking that God is going to make everything go our way, that with the true Commander in Chief in our corner, our lives will be happy and healthy and nothing will go wrong. But then life happens and jobs are lost or relationships are tested or healthy bodies get sick, and we wonder where God is and what he's doing. We wonder when his love left us.

But God's love doesn't leave us; it's our understanding of his love that is wrong. I think that life actually can be a lot harder after you commit to Christ. But there is so much more joy to be found when you're walking with God than when you're not. And it's a joy that doesn't go away. Hurts come and go, but we can still find happiness. God's love for us remains consistent.

That is why it's so important to realize that hurt *can* be good for us. First Peter 4:12–13 reminds us, "Friends, when life gets really difficult, don't jump to the conclusion that God isn't on the job. Instead, be glad that you are in the very thick of what Christ experienced. This is a spiritual refining process, with glory just around the corner."

GOD LOVES OUR TEARS

Christ was perfect, but his life wasn't. He too experienced ups and downs. Friends betrayed him, family questioned him, rulers threatened him. And he wept when he received bad news (John 11:32–35).

If we use Jesus as an example (and we should), we realize that it's okay to cry when we are hurting. We should realize that tears, an outward expression of our inward hurts, can be a treasure. I used to hate to cry, especially in church or in front of other people. It felt like such a clear sign of weakness. During our first deployment, I could be running on the treadmill at the gym and see a group of soldiers on television, and the tears would start rolling down my face. Someone would see me in the grocery store and ask about Cliff, and my eyes would instantly start to water. Sometimes it was hard to hold the tears back, but I've learned that tears are often the words our hearts can't express.

Survival Sisters
Miracles Can't Happen without the Struggles

For as long as I can remember, my grandma struggled with diabetes. When I was little I remember her pricking her finger and checking her sugar. I remember the shots she took. I always asked, "Doesn't that hurt?" She always replied, "You don't even feel it."

Over the years, my grandma continued to get worse. After dialysis and the amputation of one leg below the knee, she decided she'd had enough when the doctors asked to remove her other leg. She was done. In May of 2008, she announced she would have no more treatment of any kind.

During the struggles my grandma was having, my husband and I moved from one Army post to another, from Fort Campbell to Fort Bragg, where he joined a unit that deploys often. We had never really adjusted to his being home after he'd deployed for a year. We moved to a new duty station, a new unit, new schools, new neighborhoods, and new friends.

Somewhere among all the moving boxes, I began feeling disconnected from my husband. I was angry at him. I was angry at God. How could God let my husband be deployed for a year? How could he allow all of the chaos with moving at the same time my grandma was sick? How was that fair? Why couldn't he just let me have a break? Why couldn't he just take all the pain away?

It was on a Friday that I got the call my grandma had decided to stop all treatment. I cried and cried and wanted to be selfish and tell her not to stop until I could get there. Everyone told me it would probably be only a few days after she missed dialysis that she would pass. I knew I had to get there, but I needed to figure out how. Did I go on a plane and have Ted and the kids come by car? Did we all drive, or did I just go by myself?

That Friday I drove to the unit like I did every Friday afternoon to take the kids to karate. When Ted found me, I told him what was going on and that I had to go home. There was no way I could miss saying goodbye. I asked him what he thought we should do about travel, and the response I heard from him was, "I have to work tomorrow, so we can't leave until Sunday." I started to panic. Sunday would be too late. I needed to get there now! What Ted really said, though, was, "I am supposed to drive the bus tomorrow, but I can get someone else to do it."

Upset and feeling like Ted was putting work first, I decided to get on a plane as soon as I could leave. He would just have to figure out the kids and school and work. I was still angry with him. I was angry with him for leaving me all the time. I was angry at God for allowing it to happen.

I came home from the unit, booked a one-way ticket to Wisconsin, and packed my suitcase. While I was packing, Ted asked me if I wanted Kelly, one of our friends, to take me to the airport. He knew I was upset with him and was trying to ease my pain, but it only made me angrier. I screamed, "I want my husband to take me. I want you to show up for me. Show up for once!"

Before I left, my husband put some of my favorite Christian music on my phone so I could listen to it on the trip. My heart was heavy, knowing this would be the last time I would see my grandma. During the flight I kept praying, "God, please help heal my heart, because it's already broken." I read my Bible and marked the verses that spoke to me. I listened to my music and just prayed. I never felt closer to God, yet I still felt hurt.

My grandma was overjoyed to see me. We got to spend some good days together. During our visit, I continued to pray, but I was still angry with my husband, feeling deserted by him. One morning I heard God say, "Ted did show up for you. He's home with the kids, handling all the stuff that you normally do and his normal workload, and he hasn't complained once." It was true. If there were problems with the kids, he never let me hear that on the phone. He did show up for me.

The next seven days were both good and bad for my grandma. It was a longer journey than any of us had thought it would be. One day we were getting dinner ready and I was talking to my husband on the phone. I noticed he was very quiet. At the end of the silence, he said he was being deployed again the next month. Through my tears, I felt torn. I wanted to get on a plane home to spend as many days as I could with him and our kids, but I wanted to be there for my grandma also. I cut our conversation short and called my girlfriend, Ashley. We had been through deployment together, so she would understand. She would pray for me, as I didn't feel like I had it in me to pray. I was mad at God all over again. Mad that he had brought me peace but that just as quickly I had been shaken to the core again.

After we got off the phone, I sat in silence. It was in the silence that I heard God say that Ted's being deployed was actually an answer to prayer. I had worked most of the school year. Since I worked from home, the summer would prove difficult with four kids underfoot. But because of the extra money from Ted's deployment, we wouldn't have to change our normal routine. When you offer up a prayer to God, his answer may not be what you thought it was going to be. Ted's being deployed all summer would not have been my first choice of circumstances, but it was an answer to my prayer.

That year was the hardest year of my life and my marriage. I learned many lessons along the way, but the most profound lesson I learned is that you don't get to the miracle without struggle. A delay is not a denial, and I know God didn't forget me. There were times when I felt like my prayers were bouncing off the clouds, marked "return to sender." But God continued to meet me where I was.

The passage I read on the plane home stuck with me. Job 19:25–27: "I know that my Redeemer lives, and that in the end he will stand upon the earth. And after my skin has been destroyed, yet in my flesh I will see God; I myself will see him with my own eyes—I, and not another. How my heart yearns within me!" (NIV).

— *Shannon Burrous,*
Army wife

A reflection of the hurts we hold inside, tears remind us that we are flawed human beings. I once read a book by Craig Borlase called *The Naked Christian*. In the first chapter, he talks about how so many of us as believers put Christian celebrities on pedestals. The problem with doing so is that these celebrities often are forced to project false Christian walks—whether they intend to or not. Every hair is in place, their outfits are polished and planned by their image consultants, and you always hear about how wonderful their lives are. That is, until the news comes out about the Christian pop star who had an affair or a problem with pornography, or the pastor is forced to step down from the pulpit because of his addiction to pain killers or his embezzlement of church funds. The only tears you usually see Christian celebrities shed are the ones on television asking for your spiritual support in the form of Ben Franklins.

But contrary to what we often see in the lives of Christians we look up to, we do not have to be "in a good place" before we can receive God's love. Think of the people in the Bible who were with Jesus but were not in the nicest of circumstances. Matthew the tax collector. He was still ripping people off when Jesus told him to follow him (Matthew 9:9). And immediately, Matthew stood up and did just that, and Jesus came to his home to share a meal with him! What about the thief who was stretched out on a cross next to Jesus? He knew that his actions warranted his death, but still Jesus remembered him and let it be known he would be with him in his kingdom (Luke 23:42–43).

Our tears also remind us that we are in need. In those times, we are the most willing to receive. When life is good and things are moving along and we're walking around with smiles on our faces, how likely are we to accept someone's help? Not as likely as we would if our hearts are broken and we just can't see that it's going to get any better tomorrow. Then we would be a lot more likely to think about accepting help.

Sometimes it can be the same way with God. I think we forget that God doesn't just love our praise; he loves our tears as well. If you're generally a positive person, it's easy to come to God and say thanks. "Thank you, God, for who you are; thank you for loving me, for giving us the sunshine today, the rain, the beauty of the sunset."

How much harder it is to say, "God, I really don't want to get out of bed today. I just don't think I can face another day. God, I feel broken."

But it's that brokenness God wants to restore, and who better to restore it than the one who brought the Israelites out of captivity? The one who raised Lazarus from the dead? The one who walked on water and calmed the disciples' fears? He can do the same for us.

I believe God uses tears to get our attention. To get us to listen. Tears are a transmitter the Holy Spirit can work through to minister to our hearts. Psalm 116:8 says, "For you, O LORD, have delivered my soul from death, my eyes from tears, my feet from stumbling" (NIV). God loves our tears.

GOD USES HARD TIMES TO MAKE US STRONGER

I know it isn't easy to hear that hard times are good for you. My parents used to tell me that eating my vegetables was good for me too, but it never made them taste much better. Naturally, we want to avoid the unpleasant, the terrible, and the painful; that's probably one reason we have so many divorces in the world today, why people will change jobs more than ten times before they're in their forties,[12] and why some people seem to change churches like they change their clothes.

Look at what James says on the matter: "Consider it a sheer gift, friends, when tests and challenges come at you from all sides. You know that under pressure, your faith-life is forced into the open and shows its true colors. So don't try to get out of anything prematurely. Let it do its work so you become mature and well-developed, not deficient in any way" (James 1:2–4).

Every time I get on the treadmill to work out, I have a choice. I can choose to walk or I can choose to run. Now, I know I can walk. Walking is easy; I do that every day. And if I walk, I can still log the same distance I would if I ran. But the results are not the same. My heart rate doesn't increase, I don't burn as many calories, and ultimately, I don't work my muscles as hard as I would if I ran. The running is harder, but the results are so much better.

My marriage is much stronger today than it was when my husband and I were first married. That's because we have the bumps and bruises to show for it! No, I don't mean actual bumps and bruises, but we have been through some emotional scrapes and life-challenging obstacles along the way. With each hurdle we've jumped over together, though, we've learned to trust and rely on each other a little more and to love a little more deeply.

Our relationship with God is the same way. When we walk through the hurts with him—instead of trying to do it on our own—we see him work in our lives and in our hearts. And the next challenge we face, we're a little steadier because we have that history with our heavenly Father. We know he will catch us when we fall.

PLAYING THE BLAME GAME

When we walk through hard times we must avoid playing the blame game. Blaming is easy to do, though, isn't it? I once had a roommate in college (I'll call her Jamie) who was a professional in this game; she was that good. Whatever was happening to her that day was someone else's fault.

I will never forget the day Jamie came into the living area we all shared and announced how furious she was with her boyfriend. Jamie's birthday was coming up and her boyfriend was supposed to take her out for a special date. She had it all planned out. There would be dinner, maybe a movie, a romantic stroll afterward. The only problem—her boyfriend had to play in a baseball game that night.

Since we knew he was on scholarship for baseball, we tried to assure her: "Jamie, I'm sure he would much rather be with you; he can't help it if his baseball team has a game! Maybe you guys can go out afterward, or maybe the night before, or the night after."

Jamie stood as tall as her four-foot, six-inch frame would let her. "Oh, no! It *is* his fault!"

We looked at each other. "Why is it his fault?"

"He's the one who joined the baseball team!"

If we're not careful, we can find blame in anyone or in any situation. Take, for example, the question that the disciples asked Jesus after seeing a blind man sitting on the side of the road. They asked, "Rabbi, who sinned: this man or his parents, causing him to be born blind?" (John 9:1).

They were playing the blame game, assuming that because this man was blind, someone had done something wrong. But this is what Jesus said: "You're asking the wrong question. You're looking for someone to blame. There is no such cause-effect here. Look instead for what God can do" (verse 3).

Do you find yourself asking the wrong question often? Like, "Why did this have to happen?" "What did I do to deserve this?" "Why does everything have to go wrong all the time?" "Why is God trying to punish me with this deployment? With this permanent change of station? Why?"

These are not the questions we should be asking. Instead, we should ask, "What is God doing in my life right now? What is he trying to teach me? What is he trying to show me?"

I don't know the answer to why the recent wars our country has faced have required so many of our military families to make such great sacrifices; why marriages have been pushed to the breaking point; why service members have come home missing limbs or their former selves; why children have to get to know a parent all over again because they've been away for so long. But I do know that God wants to use those hurts and the brokenness and the sadness and the frustration to make it better. To make *us* better.

God wants to remind us we do not have to be strong on our own. He wants to show us that he is here to lean on. He wants to comfort us in ways that only he can. He wants to take our hurts and our pain and turn them into the very substance that will create a spark, igniting our hearts and our hopes in him. And not anything else. The military can't do it. The church can't do it. But God can. He can give you what no one else can—something I like to call spiritual grit.

FINDING YOUR SPIRITUAL GRIT

When we're dealing with hurts in our lives, we tend to try to pick ourselves up by the bootstraps and run through the pain. Ignore the hurting and it'll go away, right? Unfortunately, that doesn't always help.

Think about the oyster. For a pearl to be formed, it takes one tiny speck of sand to find a way in. Trying to stop the irritation, the oyster begins to coat the speck with nacre, the substance that forms the pearl. Layer after layer is created until a beautiful pearl is formed. But it wouldn't have happened had the speck, or the hurt, never happened.

I realized during our first deployment that the spiritual grit God was trying to create within me didn't necessarily involve the same process as that of the oyster making a pearl, smoothing things over and making me feel better. Instead, it was more like removing the pretty varnish to get down to the raw, untreated wood. To let God do something great in my life. And for me to stay out of the way so he could.

We're talking more sanding down than building up, more fortifying than "bless-ifying," more promise than performance, more endurance than immediate results.

Sometimes, there is no quick fix. Sometimes, it's all about the waiting. And that is when we need spiritual grit the most. When we wait, when we hang tough—knowing God is in control and he knows our hurts—that's when our spiritual grit is formed. Just like strength training builds our muscles, waiting builds our spiritual grit. And it's that grit that sands down the jagged edges of our hearts, our egos, and our human desires that prick and hurt ourselves and others.

> Still, if you set your heart on God
> > and reach out to him,
> If you scrub your hands of sin
> > and refuse to entertain evil in your home,
> You'll be able to face the world unashamed
> > and keep a firm grip on life, guiltless and fearless.
> You'll forget your troubles;
> > they'll be like old, faded photographs.
> Your world will be washed in sunshine,
> > every shadow dispersed by dayspring.
> Full of hope, you'll relax, confident again;
> > you'll look around, sit back, and take it easy.
> > > —Job 11:13–19

GOD USES DISAPPOINTMENT TO POINT US TO HIM

Disappointment forces us to look up to God, even if it's to raise our hands and ask, "Why?" What do you remember most as you look back over your life? Is it the good times, when nothing was happening and you were content? Or is it the hard times, when there were struggles and you were faced with hard choices? And do you remember just the bad times, or do you remember how those hard moments were resolved and overcome? Aren't those really the memories you hold on to the most?

Someone once said, "Disappointment to a noble soul is what cold water is to burning metal; it strengthens, tempers, intensifies, but never destroys it." It's not so much that God uses disappointment to draw us closer to him as it is that the relief or the rescue that follows keeps us focused on him.

GOD HASN'T FORGOTTEN US

When we experience hurt, we need to ask God to help us. In Luke 11:10, Jesus tells us, "Don't bargain with God. Be direct. Ask for what you need." Don't try to figure out how to fix the problem by yourself. Your solution may not be the best choice and may not even work. Instead, we need to ask God to fix our problems. And then we need to be patient enough to sit back and watch him work.

The Bible tells us that God hears our prayers and wants to give us what we need. Read what Romans 8:26–28 says: "Meanwhile, the moment we get tired in the waiting, God's Spirit is right alongside helping us along. If we don't know how or what to pray, it doesn't matter. He does our praying in and for us, making prayer out of our wordless sighs, our aching groans. He knows us far better than we know ourselves, knows our pregnant condition, and keeps us present before God. That's why we can be so sure that every detail in our lives of love for God is worked into something good."

Friend, I don't know about you, but this passage gives me hope! God hears our "wordless sighs"! He knows what we're going through, and he is not oblivious to the deep cuts in our hearts. This is why it is so important that we regularly spend time reading his Word and praying and talking with him. This is the only way we will have a life of love for God that he can transform and work into "something good."

HEARING GOD'S VOICE

We also need to listen to God, something that is difficult for most of us. I struggle with this, but when I do take the time to listen, when I do shut everything out and focus on hearing God's voice, my life is only changed for the better.

You might wonder how it's possible to hear God's voice. For me, it's not a sound but a feeling inside. When I feel convicted or have a thought that is so far out of my comfort zone, I know it can be no one else but God. We have the ability to listen for God's voice and for what he has to say to us; we also have the choice to act on what he tells us.

I learned this the hard way. One week I had been studying about prayer in my quiet time, and I was following the advice of an author who had written a book on the subject. She suggested taking a pen and a piece of paper and—in a spirit of prayer, concentrating all of my attention on God and asking him to speak to me—writing down everything that came to mind. So I did just that. And I wrote, "You are going to go through a hard time. But don't be afraid. I am with you. I want you to go to church tonight. I have a special message for you."

I didn't know what to think about this. We normally didn't go to church on Wednesday nights. Doubts immediately started firing off. What would my husband say to this? Did I really hear from God? Was I just putting words in my own head? I'm sorry to say that I got busy with other things that day and we didn't go to church that night. The next day, my husband called to tell me his job had been eliminated. I had to tell him about what I had heard God say to me the day before.

"Well, it might have been nice to know what that special message was!" he said. I had to agree!

Though we missed the "special message," we clung to the rest of what God had said. That we shouldn't be afraid, that he was with us. We had to trust that he knew what he was doing and would take care of us. And he has.

Accepting the Bad with the Good

As a military wife, I don't live on Easy Street. My neighborhood is not in Rich Estates, and my city isn't even close to Paradise Found. There are detours and bumps in the road and out-of-order traffic lights that can make the simplest, most direct route complicated. God never promised us an easy life. But he does promise that he won't leave. He won't forget. He won't turn his back. He won't allow us to be alone.

If I believe that God is with me, then I can't believe he would leave me to be poor—or rather to be "poor me." For when I allow "poor me" to come and live for the day or the week or even the month, I am turning off the hope and help that come with trusting and believing in God for everything, and I turn on the self-pity, the assumption that I deserve so much better, the whine that nothing is going my way. We have to leave the "poor me" mentality out of our lives and accept that the bad happens with the good, but it's because of the bad that the good is so appealing. What feels better—a race with no competition, or a race you fought the entire way to win? A test you aced even though you never studied for it, or a test you aced because you spent two weeks in the library reciting over and over everything you needed to know?

Deployments are not fun. Sending your husband off to war is not a happy experience. Hearing your child cry herself to sleep because she misses her daddy is one of the hardest things you'll endure. But you do go on. We need to learn to look for the good, even within the bad. What's a positive I can take away from being by myself for a year? Can I learn a new language? Discover a new hobby? Apply a new craft? Can I find ways to grow in my marriage even while we're apart? Can I grow in my faith with the extra time I have to fill? Can I ask God, when my husband comes home with symptoms of PTSD from hard combat experiences, not the question "Why?" but instead, "What are you up to? What do you want me to learn from all of this? How can I grow through all of this? How can you use me?"

Norman Vincent Peale said, "Change your thoughts and you change your world." Change your focus and you'll change your life.

STRENGTH BUILDERS

"Friends, when life gets really difficult, don't jump to the conclusion that God isn't on the job. Instead, be glad that you are in the very thick of what Christ experienced. This is a spiritual refining process, with glory just around the corner" (1 Peter 4:12–13).

"Don't bargain with God. Be direct. Ask for what you need" (Luke 11:10).

"Because you kept my Word in passionate patience, I'll keep you safe in the time of testing that will be here soon, and all over the earth, every man, woman, and child put to the test" (Revelation 3:10).

STRENGTH TRAINERS

1. What are some of the hurts you have right now? How do you cope with them?

2. Do you find yourself blaming others or blaming God for the problems you face? What is the better way to deal with disappointment?

3. How can you build up spiritual grit in your walk with God? What are some of the things you would like for him to show you?

CHAPTER EIGHT

I Can Have Joy Despite My Circumstances

★ ★ ★ ★ ★

ONE SUMMER after my freshman year in college, I came back to my hometown to be a chaperone for the youth choir tour my church was doing. Now, if you've ever been on a youth choir trip, you know the drama that can go on behind the scenes. Who is dating whom, who breaks up with whom, who isn't speaking to whom — all of the normal dynamics of teenage life.

Before we left, I decided that my job for those two weeks would be to diffuse the drama. I would focus on staying positive no matter the situation, and I would encourage others to do the same. I would keep my mind and my heart on God and what he was trying to do through this trip, and I would look out for ways that he could use me to help someone else. I was embarking on something I had never tried before. It was an experiment, and I wasn't sure what the results would be. Could I stay positive for that long? Could I really experience joy no matter what? And could I actually pass that on to others?

What I found during those two weeks really surprised me. When others were standing around, complaining and asking, "How much longer?" I felt relaxed, with a smile on my face, trying to talk to others and distract them from the long waits. When plans didn't go just right, instead of getting upset, I felt at peace, trusting that God knew something we didn't. And when one of the teenage girls turned to me one day and said, "Sara, why are you so happy? You haven't gotten upset once this whole trip!" I almost laughed out loud. I realized I had been experiencing joy despite my circumstances and it was showing! All because I took the focus off of myself and my needs and put that focus on God.

Now, I wish I could be like that all the time. It doesn't always happen. And in some seasons of life, I have to confess it's a rarity! During that time, I wasn't dealing with bills or helping my son with his homework (he wasn't born yet) or encouraging my husband to help with the chores (he was my fiancé). But all of us wrestle with hard circumstances. In the earlier chapters of this book, we talked about quite a few of the kinds of struggles we can face—deployment, loneliness, problems with finances, problems with family, difficulties with our relationships. But when we choose to experience joy over sorrow, laughter over tears, and hope over disappointment, we can embrace the lives God has for us.

I have seen a lot of tears over the last few years from military wives who are tired and worn down and worn out. But what I try to remind them—and what I'm trying to remind you—is that there is joy in life when we know Jesus. The joy is there; we only have to choose it.

In his second letter to the Corinthian church, Paul tells the Corinthians how much he longs for them to enter "this wide-open, spacious life," but he's concerned because he sees the members of the church living small, narrow lives. "Your lives aren't small, but you're living them in a small way" (2 Corinthians 6:11–12).

This is what can happen to us as we live the military life. Because we're so often pulled out of our comfort zones, we grab on to what we know. We hold on to what we can. And we live our lives in small ways. We stop risking hurt to help others, and instead, we shore up our hearts and stay in our self-made boxes, keeping our families close and others far away. We don't go to meetings on the base or the post where we live; we don't socialize with other wives from our units because we don't like the gossip that goes on; we don't socialize with other wives from our churches because we don't like the gossip that goes on there, either! So in an effort to close out everything bad, we say no, and we close out anything that could be good as well. Like making a new friend. Sharing Jesus with someone who doesn't know him. Being an encourager to someone who really needs it. We stay away from the wide-open spaces, and we miss out on the joys those spaces can bring.

We can have joy despite our circumstances, but first we must be willing to seek it out. And once we have it, living and breathing inside of us, we can't hold on to it or it will die. Joy is something that has to be shared.

KNOCKING DOWN THE WALLS

When you think of your relationship with Christ, do you feel happy? Do you feel at peace? Do you feel joyful? Most of us might say, "I feel grateful." "I feel safe." "I feel secure." But do you feel joyful?

I once read a column by a Christian professor who was criticizing two missionaries for being "too happy" and attributing the joy they felt to a simplistic and naïve conception of

Survival Sisters
There's Joy in All of It

"I've got the joy, joy, joy, joy down in my heart."

Remember that children's church song? How soon we forget. Deployment, training, missed birthdays, missed holidays, loneliness, crying. How in the world are we supposed to find joy within? We aren't ... not in the world anyway; our joy needs to come from the Lord. James 1:2 reads, "My brethren, count it all joy when you fall into various trials" (NKJV). Being a military family definitely has its share of trials, but are we controlled by our circumstances, or do we control them?

My story begins in marriage to a military man. My husband's military career was always "his thing," and for so many years it really didn't affect me. But with our country now in two wars, I realized that his military career did involve me and our children. I spent our first deployment very bitter at my husband. I felt slighted because he was without our kids and could come and go, eat, sleep, whatever, whenever he wanted. (Yeah, right ... in the middle of a war!) Consumed by my bitter thoughts, I found no joy, only resentment toward the man I loved with all my heart.

Psalm 126:5: "Those who sow in tears shall reap in joy" (NKJV). As we came to a milestone in my husband's career, I realized that I needed to accept and love his call to the military. You see, he really did feel that God wanted him as a soldier. I began to pray and to involve myself in what was going on with his job, and God began to soften me, bringing me a joy and a heart of pride for what my husband does. As we drew near to his second tour, my heart actually filled with excitement. How funny it seems now for me to describe it that way, but there is no other. I wasn't glad that he was deploying again, but I was joyful, in a manner that I could describe only as coming from the hands of Jesus.

First John 1:4: "that your joy may be full" (NKJV). As I grew, through Christ, into a proud, helpful, supportive military wife, I began volunteering to help other military families. I came to love and look forward to anything having to do with the military. My soldier puts his life on the line, puts his family on hold, but we know God called us here. We do not have perfect circumstances. I still cry when my husband is gone and I get lonely, but I know that I am never alone. My God lives in me to bring me the joy I need to rejoice despite my circumstances.

Isaiah 61:7: "Instead of your shame you shall have double honor, and instead of confusion they shall rejoice in their portion. Therefore in their land they shall possess double; everlasting joy shall be theirs" (NKJV).

I learned that if you accept what God has given you to work with, then he will bring a joyful song into your heart. It's just as Isaiah 65:18 says: "But be glad and rejoice forever in what I create" (NKJV).

— *Shauna Irigarry,*
Army National Guard wife

God. While it's true that God is holy and we should love and respect and honor that, God is about joy as well. Just look at some of the psalms we read:

> "I'm thanking you, GOD, from a full heart, I'm writing the book on your wonders. I'm whistling, laughing, and jumping for joy; I'm singing your song, High God" (Psalm 9:1–2).

> "You made me so happy, GOD. I saw your work and I shouted for joy" (Psalm 92:4).

> "We're depending on GOD; he's everything we need. What's more, our hearts brim with joy since we've taken for our own his holy name. Love us, GOD, with all you've got—that's what we're depending on" (Psalm 33:20–22).

Somewhere along our spiritual journey, we have allowed others to convince us that there is no joy in Christianity. And so when hardships come, there is no grinning and bearing it; there's just bearing it. But God wants us to be joyful! Because our joy is not based on our circumstances. It is based on the love he has for us regardless of the circumstances. When we allow joy to shine, we are holding on to the truth that "if God is for us, who can be against us?" (Romans 8:31 NIV). But when we deny ourselves the joy of being a Christ-follower, we build a wall that is hard to tear down. We become cold, hard, and impenetrable. But if we truly desire to be God Strong in everything we are and everything we do, we must have soft hearts, willing hands. We cannot let go of the knowledge that God knows—and knows us—best.

THE WALL OF APATHY

One of the walls that we build the quickest is the wall of apathy. This is the wall that says, "I don't care," and, "It doesn't bother me." When we build this wall, we think we're keeping our feelings safe and our hearts secure.

I remember talking on the phone to a military wife out of Fort Campbell one afternoon. She had a toddler and a new baby, and her husband was home on leave but getting ready to go back to Iraq. I asked her how she was doing, how they were managing, and if she had any help for after he left. She said they were fine, that no, they didn't have any family around, but she managed okay by herself. When I mentioned Wives of Faith and that she might like to get involved, she immediately said, "No, we keep to ourselves. We don't need anyone else."

We can convince ourselves that we're fine on our own. We don't care if we're by ourselves. We don't care if there are others around to help. But when we allow apathy to build, we block out the joy that could be there if that wall of apathy wasn't.

THE WALL OF DISCORD

Nothing can more quickly take away our joy than when we fight with others. Whether it's with our spouses or our family members or other military spouses, when we allow discord to creep into our relationships, we certainly can lose our joy.

I am not the best at dealing with conflict. Often my initial reaction is to walk away. But God doesn't want us to walk away; he wants us to grow by facing those conflicts and handling them the right way. If you find yourself constructing a wall of discord, ask God to help you remove it.

The Wall of Defeat

This morning, I saw a military wife's Facebook status: "I don't think I can do this for four more months." That is a hard place to be. I know exactly the feelings that wife is experiencing. I have felt them myself. But when we allow the wall of defeat to go up in our lives, when we say, "I can't do this," "I can't go on," "I can't face another day," we shut ourselves out from ever having the opportunity to see God do a successful work in us. Remember, when we say we can't, we are also saying that it's all up to us. But that's not the case at all. Tearing down the wall of defeat—choosing to find the positive and the good and the joy in each day—is vital if we want to be God Strong.

This can be hard to do. When Cliff was in Iraq, people at church asked me how I was doing. Well, there were days that were tough, but there also were days that were good. And on those days, I said, "Oh, we're doing great; everything is good!" I always got the strangest looks, because after all, I was a military wife whose husband was deployed. I couldn't possibly be happy!

To overcome feelings of defeat and hopelessness, you may have to keep at a distance others who would discourage you. Look for those friends who will encourage you, the ones who will stand at the finish line cheering you on, rather than telling you to go home. Those are the encouragers we need around us.

We can knock down all of these walls and others I didn't mention when we focus on God and not ourselves. We can experience joy when we direct our attention to God's desires and not our own. We do that by accepting what God gives us, embracing where he leads us, and understanding that both hardships and blessings come when we give our lives to him.

The Story of Joseph

If there was anyone in the Bible who had a reason to be joyless in his circumstances, it might have been Joseph. This was a man who experienced betrayal after betrayal in his life and yet still found joy and God's favor despite his situation.

Let's look briefly at the tough circumstances Joseph found himself in. (Joesph's story starts in Genesis 39.)

> *His brothers stripped him, threw him into a pit, and then sold him into slavery.* But Joseph was sold to not just anyone in Egypt but to one of Pharaoh's officials, Potiphar, the captain of Pharaoh's guard (Genesis 39:1). Genesis 39:2–4 says, "The LORD was with Joseph and he prospered.... When his master saw ... that the LORD gave him success in everything he did, Joseph found favor in his eyes" (NIV). Potiphar put Joseph in charge of his entire household. But the good life wasn't quite ready to stay.
>
> *He was accused of something he didn't do and thrown into prison.* Have you ever tried to do everything right and still found yourself on the receiving end of trouble? That was Joseph after Potiphar's wife took an interest in him. But when Joseph didn't respond to her

advances, she did what any "woman scorned" does: she got even, lying to her husband that Joseph had attacked her and watching with satisfaction as the poor guy was hauled off to prison (Genesis 39:20). Sitting in prison, Joseph might have given up. But once again, we're told that "the LORD was with him" and "showed him kindness and granted him favor in the eyes of the prison warden" (Genesis 39:21 – 22 NIV). He was put in charge of his fellow inmates and over everything that was done in the prison.

He was given a promise, and then was promptly forgotten about. For two years. Despite helping out Pharaoh's chief cupbearer, interpreting his dream as well as the chief baker's dream, Joseph did not get the good word that the cupbearer had promised to put in for him to Pharaoh. Instead, he sat for two more years in prison before he was brought out to interpret Pharaoh's own dream. That's 735 more days. Imagine counting that down!

Now, nowhere throughout the seven or eight chapters of Joseph's story does it say, "Joseph showed great joy when he was in prison." "Joseph was very excited to be sold as a slave." "Joseph didn't mind at all being lied about." But joy is not just an outward expression of feeling. Joy can be an inward state of being. One definition I saw says that "joy is a delight of the mind, from the consideration of the present or an assured approaching possession of a good."[13]

"An assured approaching possession of a good." See, I believe this is what Joseph had as he was going through all of his trials. These were tough, tough circumstances he was handed, but he never failed to remember where his focus needed to be. Who his focus needed to stay on. God was in his life and his heart and his mind every step of the way; we know this because of Joseph's response to Pharaoh when Pharaoh asked him to interpret his dream. "'I cannot do it,' Joseph replied to Pharaoh, 'but God will give Pharaoh the answer he desires'" (Genesis 41:16 NIV).

Joseph's joy came from within. It is what kept him going and kept him consistently devoted to God, and what kept God consistently devoted to Joseph. Because if you go back and look at Joseph's story, the one constant throughout his changing-from-one-extreme-to-the-next circumstances was God. He never left Joseph. His relationship to Joseph remained the same. "The Lord was with Joseph."

We need to remember that the Lord is with us too.

Why We Lose Our Joy

Before we can understand how we keep our joy, we need to understand how easily we can lose our joy if we're not careful.

We lose our joy when we try too hard on our own. I am so guilty of doing this. Do you ever find yourself just trying to make everything right? To keep all the plates spinning in the air and everything going the way you think it should be? Martha experienced this when Jesus came for a visit. She was trying so hard to make everything perfect that she missed the point. Her joy couldn't depend on a fabulous meal and perfect hostess skills; instead, she needed to take a step back, breathe in, and release some of those natural tendencies to control so she could fully experience the joy of being with Jesus.

We lose our joy when life becomes work. Have you ever reached a point where life just isn't fun anymore? Where you wonder where all the happiness has gone? Perhaps you were looking in the wrong places.

If we look back at Joseph's story, we see that his life was pretty much all about work. When he was young, he tended his father's sheep. After he was sold by his brothers, he managed his master's house and financial affairs. He directed a prison. He ultimately saved a kingdom and hundreds of thousands of lives in the process. But nowhere in that story do we see Joseph complain about the work itself. Joseph sensed that even in these harsh and demanding conditions, God was with him. He never left. So life wasn't "work" for Joseph; it was what he was supposed to do.

We lose our joy when we see all of our inadequacies. There are lots of things I can do well. But there are also a lot of things I can't! And Satan likes nothing better than to remind me of those things every chance he gets. During the writing of this book, I felt inadequate in different ways. I wondered whether active military wives will accept me and what I have to say despite my being "just" a Reserve wife. I have had my good days and my bad days because of my husband's employment situation. There are days when I know God is with us, and then there are days when I feel like shouting, "Anybody up there?" And because of our situation, I struggle to know how to prioritize everything and keep the ministry God has given me going when I'm concerned about my family's survival.

Moses felt inadequate. When God brought him forward to use him for his plan, Moses begged to get out of it not once, but several times. Moses did not have a lot of joy! All he had was the feeling that he wasn't good enough. But he was missing the point that God wants us to remember: it's not about us. We will never measure up in the ways we think we should. But our being available to let God work through us is what really counts.

LIVING WITH JOY

How different would you look if you walked around more often with a smile instead of a frown? Would it encourage others around you? Would you feel better? Would you function better? I hear and see so many wives who are struggling just to get by. They have no joy! They have no laughter! They have no peace. They are trying their hardest just to survive. They are definitely not thriving.

But if we have that relationship with Jesus, shouldn't we also have joy? No matter what? I'm not talking about being happy all the time with plastic smiles on our faces. I'm talking about a deeply rooted feeling of satisfaction, knowing that God is in our corner, holding us up.

We can rejoice that God knows what's going to happen before we do.

We can rejoice that God has saved us and wants to take each of us on an incredible journey called life.

We can rejoice that God has given us husbands to love and adventurous lives to live.

We can rejoice that God is good.

We can rejoice that no matter our sorrows, God knows our tomorrows.

We can rejoice that God is with us, and that he never leaves.

Let's discuss some more reasons why we can live in joy.

I can have joy by being content in my walk with God, knowing it is not about the destination but the journey. I once heard the story of an old dog who was watching a young dog chase his tail. The young dog stopped to rest and told the older dog, "I believe happiness is in my tail, and if I catch it, then I will have happiness!" The older, wiser dog said, "I caught mine once, and I found out that happiness is not in the catching; it's in the pursuit."

Have you ever been in the car on a long trip, just *waiting* to get to the end? The more you think about how much longer there is to go, the longer the car ride feels. You are focused on the end of the trip, and so the trip itself is meaningless to you. Just a means to the end.

But what would happen if you start looking out your window, instead of at the clock in the dashboard? Would you notice the scenery around you? Maybe the sunshine or the beautiful blue sky? Maybe you would see some funny faces or moments in the cars traveling next to you. God wants us to enjoy the moments in front of us and to experience the joy he will give us in them. But if we don't watch for them, we can miss them.

Joseph's journey led him to an incredible destination, where God used him, where he was needed most, but it was the journey that made him who he was. Joseph did not set out to rescue a people from famine *tomorrow*. Instead, he was intent on staying true to God *today*, and the next day, and the next day, and because he did so, God used him in an incredible way.

I can have joy when I look for my blessings instead of my curses. I have played a game with my son for as long as I can remember. We call it the Gratitude Game. Anytime he starts getting grumpy (usually because he isn't getting something that he wants), I tell him we have to play this game. The rules are simple: name three things that you are grateful for. This little exercise is a reminder to him of what he already has and what's really important. I find that I have to play this game myself as well. When I'm stewing over the fact that my husband is gone yet again or when there is something I want but can't have, I remind myself what I do have. And if I'm honest, I have a lot to be thankful for.

Now, I don't know if Joseph ever played the Gratitude Game, but surely he must have had moments when he wondered how he had gotten where he was. Sitting in that damp, dark prison after the chief cupbearer left him, I'm sure he must have done a lot of thinking, a lot of praying, and a lot of waiting, always wondering when the door would open and they would come for him.

Still, Joseph focused on his blessings instead of his curses. He focused on what God had done in his life rather than on what God had not done or had taken away. He recognized the blessings God put in his path and made it a point to remember them when he became a father, naming one son Manasseh, saying, "It is because God has made me forget all my trouble" (Genesis 41:51 NIV), and another son Ephraim, adding, "It is because God has made me fruitful in the land of my suffering" (verse 52 NIV).

When we remember our blessings, we forget the wrongs. We can take joy in the right.

I can have joy because God does not just restore us; he retools us through every experience we go through, good or bad. If I wanted to restore something—an old piece of furniture, for example—I would try to return that chair or table or china cabinet to its original condition. But if I wanted to retool it, I would change that piece of furniture for the better. I'd add a new cushion to the chair or a nicer finish to the table, all with the intention of improving it and making it better than it was before.

Friend, that is what God does with us. Through every circumstance we face—good, bad, or indifferent—God can use life situations to make us better. To improve us today from where we were yesterday. To bring us closer to him.

This is why we can have joy despite our circumstances. This is why we can walk with certainty into whatever life throws at us, because God is with us. As Psalm 28:7 says, he is "my strength and my shield; my heart trusts in him, and I am helped" (NIV). He has "turned my wailing into dancing"; he has taken away my mourning and instead given me joy (Psalm 30:11 NIV).

Throughout the book of Psalms, we are called on to shout for joy. Take that challenge and start it today!

Strength Builders

"This is what I want you to do: Ask the Father for whatever is in keeping with the things I've revealed to you. Ask in my name, according to my will, and he'll most certainly give it to you. Your joy will be a river overflowing its banks!" (John 16:23–24).

"He lived in alert expectation of the kingdom of God" (Luke 23:51).

"Do everything readily and cheerfully—no bickering, no second guessing allowed! Go out into the world uncorrupted, a breath of fresh air in this squalid and polluted society. Provide people with a glimpse of good living and of the living God. Carry the light-giving Message into the night so I'll have good cause to be proud of you on the day that Christ returns. You'll be living proof that I didn't go to all this work for nothing" (Philippians 2:14–16).

"Sing joyfully to the LORD, you righteous; it is fitting for the upright to praise him" (Psalm 33:1 NIV).

"For you make me glad by your deeds, O LORD; I sing for joy at the works of your hands" (Psalm 92:4 NIV).

Strength Trainers

1. What are some of the toughest challenges when it comes to having joy in your life?

2. What do we need to remember when it comes to keeping our joy active and full?

3. In what areas of your life do you need more joy? Ask God to help you with them.

CHAPTER NINE

WORSHIP LESSENS
MY WORRIES

★ ★ ★ ★ ★

One summer a few years ago, my son, Caleb, started swimming lessons. The experience wasn't exactly easy for him. Caleb is not a daredevil. I've never had to worry about him jumping out of trees and breaking legs or riding his bike full speed down a hill and breaking an arm. (Though he did fall off the monkey bars at school and broke his arm in two places ten days after Cliff came home from his first deployment.) No, Caleb certainly has no desire to take up where Evel Knievel left off. And when the other kids were diving into the pool like mini-torpedoes, my son was perfectly happy to run around to the shallow end and calmly walk down the steps, his bright yellow "wings" hugging his arms. This made his mom happy but left his dad scratching his head and thinking his son had spent too much time with Mom!

The worry began before we even got to the swim lessons that first day. "Will I have to go underwater?" Caleb asked from the back seat of the car, a concerned tone in his voice.

"I'm not sure," I told him.

"Will I have to go in the deep end?" he questioned. "Can I just use my floaties?"

By the time we actually got to the pool, worry was in full swing. He stood there looking scared and small next to the five other kids in his swim class, and it was obvious he had the least amount of experience. While the other kids jumped in and swam out and back with the instructor, Caleb hugged the wall, shaking his head decidedly no when his teacher tried to get him to come into the water with her.

Eventually he relented, but after he went in a couple of times and came back out, I saw the tears welling up and knew that a meltdown was imminent. I waved him over so I could calm him down. I mustered everything within me to give him a good pep talk, willing my "mommy" tendencies away and launching Operation WWMHS (What Would My Husband Say).

"Caleb, you can't let the pool win. *You* need to win."

"But Mom, you always tell me that winning isn't what's important."

Boy, I hate it when they actually listen!

"Yes, but Caleb, this time is different. *You* need to be the winner, not the pool. You have to beat the pool. You can't let the pool win. You can't let your worry win. If you let it win, you'll never learn to swim. You'll never have the fun you can have when you know how to swim. You have to win this time."

That's what I told him, or something to that effect. I was giving him tough love in a hard dose, and I told him he had to get back in before we left. Finally, he calmed down and went in and let the instructor help him swim across and back. He got out with a huge smile on his face. The sign of victory.

As we headed back to the car, Caleb took my hand and looked up at me, grinning from ear to ear. "Thanks, Mom, for making me get back in and helping me beat the pool. Thanks for helping me win."

There are times when winning does count, and when it comes to worry, it's imperative that we defeat it. There are many times in our lives that we can face worry, defeating thoughts, paralyzing emotions, apathetic attitudes. We can struggle to keep going and not let those feelings get the best of us.

I believe Satan would like nothing better than to use worry to distance us from everyone we love, including God. He would love to see us defeated, emotional basket cases, unable to endure. A retired military wife I know once told me how she prayed that our troops would achieve victory, not just so the war could end but so the war could be *won*, and I think the same can apply to us as military wives. We need to pray that God will give us victory in our marriages and victory in our families and victory in our daily lives. One of the ways we can experience victory daily is through the act of worship, when we honor and remember and show reverence to God.

Worry and worship can't coexist. I can't worry about what will happen tomorrow and praise God for what he's doing today. My relationship with him doesn't work like that. When our focus is on God and his being and his might, it's not on ourselves. But the opposite applies: if we are focused on ourselves and worried about what we can or can't do, then we're not focused on God, and it's harder to spend time in worship.

Keeping a mindset of worship, however, isn't as easy as keeping a mindset of worry, is it? Take, for instance, the woman who for many years couldn't sleep at night because she worried that her home would be burglarized. One night her husband heard a noise in the house, so he went downstairs to investigate. When he got there, he found a burglar. The husband said to the burglar, "Come upstairs and meet my wife. She has been waiting ten years to meet you."[14]

A real burglar can steal from you once; worry can steal from you night after night for many years. Worry can take our sleep, but it can also rob us of our health and our overall happiness. And yet, if we're not careful, the habit of worrying becomes so familiar to us that it's hard to give up.

The Worries of a Military Wife

The worries of a military wife aren't entirely different from the worries of other women or other wives. We worry about the future—our children's future, our marriage's future—and we often worry that the past will catch up with us. We get anxious about the safety of our husbands, the stability of our families, the security of our homes. We worry about wounds, seen and unseen. We worry that things won't ever be the same; we worry that they just might never change.

There is a lot we can worry about if we allow ourselves to! When we let worry creep into our lives, it can be a lot like the man who once tried pushing a wheelbarrow up a mountain. In his wheelbarrow he had two rocks he was taking up to the top of the mountain. But as he got higher and higher, he picked up more rocks. He didn't have to—these were extra rocks. But it didn't matter; he picked them up and put them in his wheelbarrow to carry as well. Well, of course, the more rocks he collected, the heavier his wheelbarrow grew and the harder it was to keep going. He pushed that

Survival Sisters
My Prayer to God

As I write this, my husband, Joe, is at the end of a fifteen-month deployment to Iraq. It's the longest time we've been apart, and it has been hard for us and our three children. I've been looking back at some of the journal entries I've kept during this time. Here's one entry I wrote around the halfway mark of this journey:

During my personal quiet times, I've been working my way through the book of Isaiah. This last week has been a particularly tough one for me, especially with our eight-year-old son, and the following verses ministered to my aching soul in a powerful way:

Strengthen the weak hands,
and make firm the feeble knees.
Say to those who have an anxious heart,
"Be strong; fear not!
Behold, your God
will come with vengeance,
with the recompense of God.
He will come and save you."

Then the eyes of the blind shall be opened,
and the ears of the deaf unstopped;
then shall the lame man leap like a deer,
and the tongue of the mute sing for joy.
For waters break forth in the wilderness,
and streams in the desert;
the burning sand shall become a pool,
and the thirsty ground springs of water.
—Isaiah 35:3–7 ESV

How my heart needed to be reminded of this today, God. My hands have felt weak lately during this deployment, and here at the six-month mark, I feel as though parts of my life are threatening to unravel and I am so inadequate to face the many more long months and challenges solo. And it's not just my own heart that hangs in the balance but also the hearts of my three children and my soldier-husband. All the deep needs and aching fears seem beyond me to address, and I feel that I can't continue to "hold it all together" and to effectively love each of them through this as I should.

Am I parenting and disciplining right? Am I showing Joe enough love and support in my communication with him? Am I handling our finances well enough? Am I taking care of our home properly and making good decisions when problems arise? Am I involved enough in my kids' schools, active in my church, in my neighborhood, and with the other wives in Joe's unit? Has my correspondence been enough for family and friends? Am I taking care of my health and staying on top of all the doctor, dentist, and orthodontist appointments and parent-teacher conferences for my kids? Am I making the right choices when so many of those choices I am forced to make alone? How do I do all this, God?

I find myself so fearful and overwhelmed today—caught up in the "what ifs" of this difficult place. Sometimes I physically feel as though I am about to collapse under the weight of all this pressure!

And then your Word breaks through to my heart once more and gives me hope, heavenly Father. Not just conjured optimism, but real, genuine hope. An assurance and a confident expectation that my weary heart was lacking this day.

You draw me close and you remind me that you equip me daily with the strength that I need—all of it. It is you, God, who comes to my rescue. If I did not need saving, then how could I know you as my great and faithful Savior?

When I look at what I am facing these fifteen months, it seems insurmountable to me. My children—especially my little boy—are hurting so deeply. It seems impossible for me to patch the gaping hole of their father's absence.

As I turn back to this passage in Isaiah, something strikes me about verses 5 and 6. The conditions being described here—blindness, lameness, a desert wasteland—are not just problematic to correct; they are seemingly impossible to cure. Enter our God, whose specialty is accomplishing the impossible and applying his power and promises to our faith. What are the results? The blind now see, the deaf now hear, the lame can leap, the mute sing for joy, and there are streams of precious water flowing in this desert, collecting in pools, springing up from the earth, quenching the thirsty ground and easing the burn. What was parched and dry and hopeless has become a place of refreshing, healing, and new promise.

Oh, my Rock, I know you are breaking forth in my wilderness. I know you are bringing the rain. Help me to rejoice in your promise. Help me to trust and hold my heart steady. My hope is in you, God.

— *Kristen Huggins,*
Army wife

enormous load for as long as he could, but finally, the man saw a bench where he could sit and rest for a minute. That's when God asked him a question.

"Why are you so tired?"

"Well, God, it's because I'm trying to take these rocks up to the top of the mountain."

"Did you start out with all of those?"

"Well, no, God. But I saw those other rocks and thought that I should do something with them too. Somebody needed to."

"But did *you* need to?"

The man hesitated. "Well ..."

God spoke gently. "The burdens you are carrying are not yours. They are mine. So let me carry them for you."

How often do you carry worries and burdens that aren't yours to lug?

When we allow worry to control our thoughts, our emotions and our bodies are sure to be next. Worry and stress can wreak havoc in our hearts and lives. Like a virus, they can consume us. But Jesus said, "Come to me, all you who are weary and burdened, and I will give you rest" (Matthew 11:28 NIV).

A small group of wives had joined me at my house one night to connect. We shared a short devotional together, and as often happens, we all ended up around the kitchen table, talking and laughing and sharing our thoughts and experiences. None of these women had known each other very long. We all had different backgrounds; some of us were active Army or active Navy; others were Reserve or Guard. Some of us had husbands who were deployed, a few had husbands getting ready to go, and one had a husband just return. A few were strong in their faith; at least one was a brand new Christian. Even though there were differences, there were still a lot of commonalities among us, and worry was one of them. One by one, each of us opened up about some of the things that were bothering us.

One young wife, married only a few years, whose husband had been deployed for just about as many, opened up about her frustration in trying to get pregnant.

"We tried while he was home last year, but it didn't happen, and four months later, he had to leave again. It's hard to start a family when half of you isn't there!" she said, the tears starting to fall. As the rest of us grabbed tissues and handed them to her, she continued to cry. "I'm starting to wonder if I will ever be a mom."

This is one worry that hurts the hearts of a lot of military wives; life gets put on hold, and many wonder if the "play" button will ever get pushed again as long as they're in the military.

Hannah of the Old Testament could relate to that young wife at my kitchen table that night. We find Hannah's story in the first chapter of 1 Samuel. For years and years, she had begged God for a child. Holding a little one in her arms was the cry of her heart, and she worried that she might never see her dream realized. Standing before God, praying and crying out through her grief and hurt, Hannah looked to him for help. She was upset; she didn't understand why God hadn't answered her prayer, but she kept praying. Hannah kept worshiping. The Bible says she poured out her soul to God (1 Samuel 1:15). And that is what we must do.

The Importance of Worship

When we worship God, we show him the attention he deserves. If you've grown up in church, you may think of worship as just the singing time during a church service on Sunday morning. But worship is more than that. To know God, we must spend time with him; worshiping him is more than just making sure we take part in the spiritual food groups of prayer, Bible reading, and church attendance. We must live God's truth and follow God's will, day after day. We must meet him each day, not on our terms but on his. Worshiping God is less about location and more about restoration—restoring our connection with him daily, keeping the lines of communication open with the one who matters most.

When I was in Iraq in November of 2003, I had the opportunity to visit an Iraqi Christian church in the middle of Baghdad. The congregation met in an old Anglican church building that had been there since the late 1800s. Before the war started, the pastor of the church had run a Christian tape ministry out of his home, taping sermons he heard on the radio and distributing them to whoever would listen. Saddam's men discovered that all over Iraq, secret groups of people who were abandoning Islam and embracing Christianity were listening to this pastor's tapes. Because this was seen as a threat to Saddam's power and influence in the Muslim world, the pastor was arrested and imprisoned until US and coalition forces took over the city.

This church didn't have much by American standards—an electric keyboard instrument accompanied their singing, and the congregation sat in rows of white plastic lawn chairs. But as I listened to them singing a familiar song, but in a different language, it struck me how free these people were at this moment. There were men and women both, standing, raising their hands, their eyes closed, with smiles on their faces, worshiping the living God. Without fear. Without worry. Without consequence. Looking at their environment, one might have thought they didn't have much, but when you looked at their countenances, it was plain that their joy was full. They had everything in the world because they had Jesus.

The contrast couldn't have been more obvious — or tough to take — when I was home the following week and standing in my own church service, with a big stage, bright lights, large video screens, and all of the technical advances you could imagine. I felt so guilty. How often had I stood there previous Sundays, sometimes tired, wishing I could be back in my warm comfy bed or thinking about how lunchtime couldn't come soon enough? But then I thought back to those Iraqi families in that church service, in a building with no heat, sitting in those hard, white plastic chairs. So many of the congregation were women whose husbands, fathers, or grandfathers had been killed in previous wars or had left the country in search of work to send money home to their families.

One man I talked to, Firas, had lived during three wars. He was a child during the Iran-Iraq war, he was a teenager during the Gulf War, and at the beginning of the Iraq war, he was an adult with his own family. He told me how he had been on the internet and learned that people all over the world were praying for the 10/40 window (countries in the area between 10 and 40 degrees north of the equator), the area of the world where he lived. He said that those prayers were being answered with the freedom Iraq was now experiencing. And though that freedom was uncertain at best, still he and the rest of the congregation raised their hands and worshiped, grateful and excited to be in God's house. In God's presence.

We need to be excited to be in God's presence! We need to soak in him, experience him, and remain in him. Only through God and his presence do we receive strength. We receive his love and his encouragement. Which is a better source of power? A cell phone's battery or a cell phone's charger? Eventually the battery runs out. But a phone plugged into its charger could potentially keep on going indefinitely. When we are intentional about our times of worship, we too can keep going for much longer than we anticipate. If we aren't, as A. W. Tozer said, "Without worship, we go about miserable."

PERSONAL WORSHIP

Prayer and Bible study are important in our personal worship of God, but so often we neglect these valuable faith-builders. And they are valuable. It's hard to fear when you're asking God for his help. It's hard to worry when you're reading God's promises. Paul underscores the importance of prayer in his letter to Timothy. He writes, "Since prayer is at the bottom of all this, what I want mostly is for men to pray — not shaking angry fists at enemies but raising holy hands to God. And I want women to get in there with the men in humility before God, not primping before a mirror or chasing the latest fashions but doing something beautiful for God and becoming beautiful doing it" (1 Timothy 2:8–10).

How often do we focus our energy on those things Paul talks about, instead of focusing it on God? Maybe we're not "primping," as Paul puts it, but we're fretting. We're looking at everything but God.

I know this was the case for me during our deployment. I focused on exercise and blamed neglectful friends for my problems, instead of asking God to take what I was dealing with and do something to make it beautiful. To do something to bring glory to him.

Jaylene, an Army wife, wrote me through Facebook about a blessing God had given her: "You know, just when I want to throw in the towel and let myself have a 'bad' day, God answers a prayer and it humbles me and causes me to thank him for his grace. Last night as I was falling asleep, I asked the Lord if I could talk to my husband before Sunday. And at 7:00 a.m. this morning, I got a phone call from my husband. Turns out one of his battle buddies was preparing to leave today for AIT [advanced individual training], so this buddy asked if my husband would like to give me a quick call before he left. Praise the Lord! It's the little answers to prayer that really make God real to me in everyday life."

What a great truth. "It's the little answers to prayer that really make God real to me in everyday life." This is what worship is all about; seeing God not only in the horrific but also in the ho-hum. Not just the battles with giants but the feeding of a hungry crowd. God provides the answers to prayers big and small.

Jesus told the Samaritan woman at the well, "It's who you are and the way you live that count before God. Your worship must engage your spirit in the pursuit of truth. That's the kind of people the Father is out looking for: those who are simply and honestly *themselves* before him in their worship" (John 4:23).

God does not expect us to be people we aren't. And he doesn't want us to come to him with only the positive highlights. He does want us to be the children he made, and he wants us to walk in his steps.

Ways to Grow in Personal Worship

Study God's Word! Pick up a Bible and start reading. If the translation you have is difficult, find another one that is easier for you. I have several different translations, ranging from the New International Version to *The Message* to the New Living Translation and even *The Amplified Bible*, and it can be very helpful to check a few different ones when you're studying a particular passage. (There is also www.biblegateway.com if you like the ease of an electronic format.) Get a study Bible that has a good concordance and notes on the background of what you're reading. You'll be amazed at what God can use to remind you of an important truth or gift in your life.

Keep a praise and worship journal. I have a little book that I use to record what Scriptures I read each day and note anything I feel God is trying to show me or tell me. Sometimes I write my prayers down, which is great for referring to later to see how God has answered them. You can also include a section to write down what you're grateful for each day.

Start in the middle. If you're not sure where to start reading the Bible, begin with the gospel of John. Or the book of Psalms or Proverbs. You don't necessarily have to read the Bible in order, though many people prefer that. Read to learn, and read to see what God wants to say to you through what you're reading. Write down questions that come to mind, and don't be afraid to investigate those questions using a concordance or other reference material. A preacher's daughter once told me that after she'd gone to college, her mother was appalled to learn that her daughter's Bible teacher was encouraging them to ask questions. She couldn't see the difference between asking questions and *questioning* the Bible. But asking questions is how we learn and grow, gaining understanding of what God has done for us and continues to do.

Don't give up. Too often, we treat our quiet times like spiritual diets — the first time we slip up, we give up! But as my pastor reminds us frequently, if you aren't able to spend time with God today, do it tomorrow. And if it has been three days since you spent time with God, do it the next day. But don't quit! See, diets don't work because we aren't committed to the process that's required for the desired change. But spending time with God should not be just

an item on your to-do list. You should want to
spend time with him, and you *need* to spend
time with him! (And friends, if you're a military
wife, you *really do need* to spend time with him!)

CORPORATE WORSHIP

Wives of Faith recently conducted an informal survey of
one of our local chapters. One of the questions we asked
is whether the military wife is involved in a church and,
if so, whether it is a good church that is supportive of her.
While a little more than half of those who responded said
that yes, they were involved in a church, the other half
indicated that they either were not involved in a church
or didn't go regularly. This is a hard place to be, because
we need the support of other Christians! Just as we do
better in a race when others are running with us, we do
better in our spiritual walk when we have other believers
around us, encouraging and inspiring and motivating us
to keep going. And if you are reading this and are not yet
a believer, church is a great place to answer all of the questions you may have.

The book of Acts shows us the importance of corporate
worship. The early church was a family; they ate together,
worshiped together, and took care of one another's needs.
Here's a description: "They devoted themselves to the apostles' teaching and to the fellowship, to the breaking of bread
and to prayer. Everyone was filled with awe, and many won-
ders and miraculous signs were done by the apostles. All
the believers were together and had everything in common.
Selling their possessions and goods, they gave to anyone as

he had need. Every day they continued to meet together in the temple courts. They broke bread in their homes and ate together with glad and sincere hearts, praising God and enjoying the favor of all the people. And the Lord added to their number daily those who were being saved" (Acts 2:42–47 NIV).

Unfortunately, churches today are not always like that. There are some wonderful church families out there who actively support our troops and the families who serve on the home front. However, many churches are unsure how to help military spouses or families cope with the many challenges of military life. Wives may feel lost in church without their husbands next to them, or they may feel no one understands the challenges their families face.

So what's a spouse to do? Do you quit church altogether? Do you simply rely on your personal worship times to get you through?

Quitting church isn't the answer, because just as personal worship plays an important part in spiritual growth, so does worshiping with the body of believers. We won't be worshiping by ourselves in heaven, so we may want to get used to worshiping with others while we're here on earth!

Hebrews 10:25 says, "Let us not give up meeting together, as some are in the habit of doing, but let us encourage one another—and all the more as you see the Day approaching" (NIV).

One of the ways Satan kicks us when we're down is to make us think that no one, not even other believers, really cares about us. If he can cut our line to the body of Christ, then he has an advantage in causing us despair, heartache, and pain. Don't let him win! We need to push our way back into that pew or that chair and recognize that just as God will show us things at home in our prayer closets, he can also show us things as we worship and share with others.

Ways to Improve Corporate Worship Time

Find a church that is right for you. Too often, we go to a church because it's the one we grew up in or it's close to our home or someone told us it was the one we should try first. I know how hard it can be to visit different churches and how you can find yourself wishing that you can just belong *somewhere.* But you need to be in a body of believers where you will grow in your understanding and walk with God, where you can be ministered to, but also where you will be encouraged to minister to others. Too often, we find it easier just to show up, and we avoid being involved. But part of corporate worship includes the service you bring to it, either through sharing your gifts and talents or just a willingness to help.

Get connected with others in your church. Most churches have small groups, either on Sunday mornings or on certain nights of the week. If your husband is not with you, it can be intimidating to be part of this type of group, but don't talk yourself out of it. You may find a family you never knew you had, one that will pray for you and challenge you to grow in your walk with God.

Ask God for wisdom. Ask God to help you learn something about him and about yourself each time you're with other believers, whether that's in Sunday school, worship, or small group Bible study.

CONNECTING TO GOD THROUGH WORSHIP

So often we seem to try to sidestep around God. We make things more complicated than they actually are. God just wants a relationship with us. I say "just," but really, it's much more than that. He wants all of me, and he wants all of you. He wants less "doing" and more "being." And yet, we are much more willing to go to group meetings or Bible studies or church events to talk *about* God than to actually sit down and talk *to* God.

For a local Wives of Faith meeting, I once tried to schedule a prayer time, just a chance for the ladies to come together and pray—pray for each other, pray for their families, for their husbands, for our military, our country, our country's leaders. Out of a group of about fifteen to twenty wives, only one other person came. We talked a little bit about why it's so hard for many people to be in a setting like that. I too am not always completely comfortable praying out loud. When we're in a situation like that, we tend to think more about the people around us than the recipient of our prayers. We worry that our words will come out wrong or that they'll sound silly.

But prayer and worship do not have to be presented perfectly or with beautiful or flowery words. That time you spend with God simply needs to come from the heart, no matter who is around to hear it. Perfection is not required. Honesty and availability are what God looks for.

Pastor John Piper once said, "Missions is not the ultimate goal of the church. Worship is. Missions exists because worship doesn't."

Be willing to allow God to stretch and shape you through worship. Give him your worries and hold on to his love.

STRENGTH BUILDERS

"In the same way, prayer is essential in this ongoing warfare. Pray hard and long. Pray for your brothers and sisters. Keep your eyes open" (Ephesians 6:18).

"But the time is coming—it has, in fact, come—when what you're called will not matter and where you go to worship will not matter. It's who you are and the way you live that count before God. Your worship must engage your spirit in the pursuit of truth. That's the kind of people the Father is out looking for: those who are simply and honestly *themselves* before him in their worship. God is sheer being itself—Spirit. Those who worship him must do it out of their very being, their spirits, their true selves, in adoration" (John 4:23–24).

"There's more to come: We continue to shout our praise even when we're hemmed in with troubles, because we know how troubles can develop passionate patience in us, and how that patience in turn forges the tempered steel of virtue, keeping us alert for whatever God will do next. In alert expectancy such as this, we're never left feeling shortchanged. Quite the contrary—we can't round up enough containers to hold everything God generously pours into our lives through the Holy Spirit!" (Romans 5:3–5).

STRENGTH TRAINERS

1. Why is worship so important?

2. Why do worship and worry mix as well as oil and water?

3. What is the difference between personal and corporate worship? Why are both necessary?

4. Is there anything about personal or corporate worship that is difficult for you? Write these challenges down and ask God to help you overcome them so your worship to him will be sweeter and purer.

5. How can you make worship a vital part of your life from here on out?

CHAPTER TEN

I Find My
Hope in Christ

★ ★ ★ ★ ★

EVER WISH THAT GETTING HOPE was as easy as drinking milk? For many years, we've seen the commercials and the advertisements for the popular "Got milk?" campaign, which promotes the benefits of drinking cow's milk. We've seen celebrities wear milk moustaches. We've seen the funny but relatable moments of people eating peanut butter or chocolate cake with no milk to wash it down with. These ads always end with "Got milk?" You're asked the question, Do you have the one thing that will keep you strong, keep you moving, keep you happy, and keep you going?

Well, do you? Do you have hope? For out of all of the truths we've discussed up to this point, the one truth that is the basis for all of the other truths that make us God Strong is the hope we have in Jesus Christ. He is our hope! He is what keeps us strong and keeps us moving. He brings us happiness, and he is the one who keeps us going when we're not so sure we can.

There are two ways we can look at the word *hope*.

There's the verb form, "to hope." When we hope for something, we look forward to it. It's a desire that comes with reasonable confidence that it will happen or will be the way we expect it to be. When we hope, we believe in something. We put our trust in it. If I sit down in a chair, I'm hoping that it's going to hold me and not break! I trust that the chair is going to support me.

There's an old *Peanuts* cartoon that gives a good illustration of hope. Lucy and Linus are sitting in front of the television set when Lucy says to Linus, "Go get me a glass of water."

Surprised, Linus says, "Why should I do anything for you? You never do anything for me."

"On your seventy-fifth birthday," Lucy promises, "I'll bake you a cake."

Linus gets up and heads to the kitchen. "Life is more pleasant when you have something to look forward to," he declares.

Hope does give us something to look forward to. We hope that the deployment passes quickly; we hope our husbands get home soon; we hope our children do well in school; we hope that spring will come quickly and the sunshine returns to push away the cloudy grey so we can enjoy some bright blue skies.

But *hope* is also a noun. We're talking about a person or a thing in which our expectations are centered. After birds collided with his plane, taking out both engines shortly after takeoff, the pilot who successfully landed his commercial jet in New York City's Hudson River was the hope of those passengers who depended on him to save their lives. Policemen and firefighters were the hope of those who were trying to make it out of the World Trade Center towers on 9/11.

But out of all our hopes, our biggest hope, and I would say our only hope, is in Jesus Christ. He *is* our hope. He is the one our expectations are focused on. He is who we look forward to seeing one day. We are expecting him; we are trusting him. Paul calls Jesus "our living hope" (1 Timothy 1:1), and Isaiah says that "the mere sound of his name will signal hope" (Matthew 12:21).

But perhaps you're reading this and not feeling very hopeful. You may, instead, be feeling quite hopeless. I've been there! But these are exactly the times we need to remind ourselves of times when Jesus has brought hope and realize that if he has brought hope to others, he can bring that same hope to us.

Throughout the New Testament, we see many examples of the hope Jesus offered to people through his words and through his miracles. He interacted with everyone: children, townspeople, those suffering from leprosy, those suffering from greed. He gave parents back their children and healed the blind, the sick, and the demon-possessed. He brought hope to women in a time when women were rarely appreciated.

Military wives can sometimes feel unappreciated and alone; we try so hard to do so much for our families, and if we do not feel forgotten by our husbands (which I hope we do not), then quite often we still feel forgotten by the military. But Jesus hasn't forgotten us, and he offers us the same hope he offered to women in the Bible. Let's take a look at a few of these women.

THE HOPE OF PROMISES KEPT

Anna was a widow for almost her entire adult life, having been married only seven years before her husband died. For the rest of her life, she stayed in the temple, worshiping day and night, fasting and praying (Luke 2:37). She was eighty-four years old the day Mary and Joseph walked into the temple courts with Jesus to dedicate him to the Lord, as was the custom. We don't know much about Anna; she is mentioned only in this one passage of Luke. But we can assume from Simeon's account that she too had been waiting to see the Messiah, the Hope, because we're told that after she saw Jesus, she "spoke about the child to all who were looking forward to the redemption of Jerusalem" (verse 38 NIV).

God keeps his promises. His Word is filled with them. "But whoever listens to me will live in safety and be at ease, without fear of harm" (Proverbs 1:33 NIV). "This is the confidence we have in approaching God: that if we ask anything according to his will, he hears us" (1 John 5:14 NIV). "But I will see you again and you will rejoice, and no one will take away your joy" (John 16:22 NIV).

When we are struggling with the unknown and dealing with big question marks in our spirits, we need to turn to the Bible and read and reread God's promises. We can be hopeful—expecting and trusting—that what he says is true.

THE HOPE OF NO MORE SUFFERING

She had struggled with the disease for more than twelve years. For more than a decade, this woman had hemorrhaged, and no one knew how to stop it. She'd seen doctor after doctor, but without the result she hoped for. Her disease was almost as bad as leprosy, except lepers at least could be with each other. Her disease marked her as "unclean," and she had no friends and no husband, at least as far as we can infer from Scripture. This woman had spent all of her money trying to find a cure, and she was desperate. If she could just touch Jesus, she knew she would be healed, so great was her faith, and her hope, in him.

And that's exactly what happened. Mark 5:25–34 tells us that the woman, pushing her way through a large crowd that surrounded Jesus, managed to get close enough to touch his robe. Instantly, she felt one hundred percent better. She knew she'd been healed.

But then something interesting happened. Jesus turned and looked for her. "Who touched me?" he asked. When she acknowledged what she'd done, he commended her, saying, "Daughter, your faith has healed you. Go in peace and be freed from your suffering" (verse 34 NIV).

Jesus gives us hope that any suffering we face ultimately will end, whether here on earth or in heaven with him. Quite often, though, that hope requires some risk, stepping out in faith to believe that he will do what he says, and holding to that faith and to that hope however long it takes. This woman endured her pain for twelve years. How long can you trust and keep your hope alive that God will one day answer you?

The Hope of New Beginnings

The consequences of sin, whether by your own choices or the choices of others, can feel so hopeless. When sin enters the picture, it is easy to want to give up and hide away from everything and everyone. Perhaps the Samaritan woman felt this way as she made her daily walk to the well, her village's main source of water. We can assume that she made her trip to the well at high noon to avoid the other women, who usually came in the evening when it was cooler. She came during the middle of the day, the hottest part, more willing to put up with the baking sun than the icy stares and the not-so-subtle whispers about her.

She expected the heat and looked forward to the solitude, but she was surprised when she saw a man sitting by the well. And not just any man. She could tell right away by his dress that he was a Jew, and she braced herself for whatever mean-spirited treatment was coming. After all, Jews didn't like her people and never associated with Samaritans, since they thought of them as "unclean."

But he surprised her when he asked her for a drink of water (John 4:7). Jewish men certainly didn't talk to Samaritan women. And they definitely wouldn't touch a cup or anything else that was touched by a Samaritan. Clearly, this man was different.

Her curiosity now awakened, she asked him how he could ask something like that of her. Let's read the rest of the conversation.

> The Samaritan woman, taken aback, asked, "How come you, a Jew, are asking me, a Samaritan woman, for a drink?" (Jews in those days wouldn't be caught dead talking to Samaritans.)
>
> Jesus answered, "If you knew the generosity of God and who I am, you would be asking *me* for a drink, and I would give you fresh, living water."
>
> The woman said, "Sir, you don't even have a bucket to draw with, and this well is deep. So how are you going to get this 'living water'? Are you a bet-

ter man than our ancestor Jacob, who dug this well and drank from it, he and his sons and livestock, and passed it down to us?"

Jesus said, "Everyone who drinks this water will get thirsty again and again. Anyone who drinks the water I give will never thirst—not ever. The water I give will be an artesian spring within, gushing fountains of endless life."

The woman said, "Sir, give me this water so I won't ever get thirsty, won't ever have to come back to this well again!"

He said, "Go call your husband and then come back."

"I have no husband," she said.

"That's nicely put: 'I have no husband.' You've had five husbands, and the man you're living with now isn't even your husband. You spoke the truth there, sure enough."

"Oh, so you're a prophet! Well, tell me this: Our ancestors worshiped God at this mountain, but you Jews insist that Jerusalem is the only place for worship, right?"

"Believe me, woman, the time is coming when you Samaritans will worship the Father neither here at this mountain nor there in Jerusalem. You worship guessing in the dark; we Jews worship in the clear light of day. God's way of salvation is made available through the Jews. But the time is coming—it has, in fact, come—when what you're called will not matter and where you go to worship will not matter.

"It's who you are and the way you live that count before God. Your worship must engage your spirit in the pursuit of truth. That's the kind of people the

Father is out looking for: those who are simply and honestly *themselves* before him in their worship. God is sheer being itself—Spirit. Those who worship him must do it out of their very being, their spirits, their true selves, in adoration."

The woman said, "I don't know about that. I do know that the Messiah is coming. When he arrives, we'll get the whole story."

"I am he," said Jesus. "You don't have to wait any longer or look any further."

—John 4:9–26

The Samaritans differed from the Jews in their spiritual beliefs because they read only the Pentateuch, which is the first five books of the Bible as we know it today. They did not accept the rest of the Scriptures, which meant that though they worshiped the true God, they were missing much, and so they knew very little about him. Jesus was offering to this woman not only a new life but a new way to look at life.

There are a few points we can take away from this conversation. First, none of us are so badly damaged that we aren't worthy of Jesus' time. The reason Jesus asked this woman about her husband is because he already knew that she had been married multiple times and that she wasn't married to the man she was living with. Yet that didn't stop him from talking to her; it didn't stop him from offering her the greatest gift he could give her. No matter how much baggage you think you have in your life, in your past, or in your heart, Jesus loves you and he wants a relationship with you. Whether you've had that relationship before and let it fade away or you've never taken the step to start that relationship, Jesus is there, waiting at the well of our lives, offering "living water."

The "living water" Jesus offers is eternal life. The Greek word in verse 10 is actually used only in the gospel of John, and it emphasizes God's grace through Christ.[15] Jesus is God's hope for the world.

Probably feeling stung and shocked that this man knew so much about her personal life, the Samaritan woman almost seems to pick a fight when she questions Jesus on a controversial point of her day—where the right location was to worship God. The Samaritans believed it should be on a certain mountain; the Jews believed it should be Jerusalem. But as Jesus pointed out, location has nothing to do with real worship. What's much more important is where worship resides in our hearts and in our lives. "It's who you are and the way you live that count before God. Your worship must engage your spirit in the pursuit of truth. That's the kind of people the Father is out looking for: those who are simply and honestly *themselves* before him in their worship" (John 4:23).

We do not have to be perfect to come before God. We don't have to have everything together before we can start going to church. If there is any hope we can take away from the conversation between Jesus and the Samaritan woman, it's that Jesus offers new beginnings for all of us. We must only be willing to start.

The Hope of Eternity

They were two women with very different backgrounds, but they shared much more than their names. Mary, the mother of Jesus, and Mary Magdalene, a woman who helped in

Survival Sisters
Strength from Weakness

My struggles stemmed from constant health problems. Prior to my husband's deploying, I was diagnosed with a goiter in the right lobe of my thyroid, and my health was deteriorating.

A few weeks after Shawn's unit began mobilization training, I came down with a severe case of strep throat. It hit me over the weekend when my doctor's office wasn't open, and having spent too much time in a hospital, I refused to go to the ER to get slapped with a huge bill for strep throat. I called on some friends to help out, but only a few were able to do anything for me. I despised the National Guard at that time for taking my husband away when I needed him most.

My only true shoulder to lean on was Jesus' shoulder. I spent a lot of time ranting and crying, knowing God was a better listener than anyone else. I had to keep up a good front, couldn't let people see how much I hated this sacrifice. Monday rolled around and I got into my doctor's office. Now on antibiotics, I bounced back. Thankfully none of my four children contracted it from me.

Two days later I received an unexpected phone call from Shawn. Apparently word reached him that I was sick. His platoon sergeant got him a cell phone and made him call me. I later learned that when he heard how sick I was, his whole body began to shake and fear coursed through him. He didn't calm down until he heard my voice and knew that I was fine. This was one of those rare times when unit rumors actually helped to connect a husband and wife! But it was truly God's hand, because Shawn was out in FOB (forward operating base) running situational drills. At that time there was no communication. The soldiers were training, so they didn't have time to call or email.

Throughout the next year I would spend most of my time either sick or recovering. Stress from being the only parent triggered the health problems. I took a heavy dose of learning to let go and let God control the situation. I've been a Christian my entire life, yet I struggled with controlling the world around me. Shawn's deployment forced me to learn that I had no control; this was out of my hands.

Also, during the deployment, I learned the true meaning of grace. God loves us, and nothing we do can change that. Trying to control our lives to make us better as Christians only leads to failure. This step toward release helped me see the bigger picture of Jesus' sacrifice. The Scripture passage I clung to during this time has become my life's verse: "But he said to me, 'My grace is sufficient for you, for my power is made perfect in weakness.' Therefore I will boast all the more gladly about my weaknesses, so that Christ's power may rest on me. That is why, for Christ's sake, I delight in weaknesses, in insults, in hardships, in persecutions, in difficulties. For when I am weak, then I am strong" (2 Corinthians 12:9–10 NIV).

My strength to cope, move on, and give my all comes from my weakness, and only then am I strong enough. After Shawn returned home, his aunt told him that I had matured a lot during his deployment. And I had in more ways than one. My faith in God had matured. Now when I read the Bible, I see it with new eyes. What didn't make sense before is crystal-clear now, and this has made me a more understanding wife. It's easy to think that as a National Guard wife, you don't have to deal with the same problems as regular Army wives. We do; we have just as much weight on our shoulders, but we lack the constant contact with other wives in the same situation. There is no base to fix the little problems. In some cases we are solely dependant on civilians, people who don't understand exactly what it is we're going through. For me, I realized that I had a common denominator when talking with my nonmilitary friends: God.

— *Winter Peck*,
Army National Guard wife

Jesus' ministry, both had the opportunity to see the hope of Christ up close in an incredible way.

First, there was Mary, the mother of Jesus. How amazed and terrified she must have been the day an angel appeared before her and told her she was going to be the mother of God's Son. I'm sure that as she was planning her wedding to Joseph, "giving birth to the Messiah" was not on her to-do list! However, God had a plan, and Mary was an important part of it. Let's look at Luke 1:28–33:

> Upon entering, Gabriel greeted her:
>
> > Good morning!
> > You're beautiful with God's beauty,
> > Beautiful inside and out!
> > God be with you.
>
> She was thoroughly shaken, wondering what was behind a greeting like that. But the angel assured her, "Mary, you have nothing to fear. God has a surprise for you: You will become pregnant and give birth to a son and call his name Jesus.
>
> > He will be great,
> >   be called 'Son of the Highest.'
> > The Lord God will give him
> >   the throne of his father David;
> > He will rule Jacob's house forever—
> >   no end, ever, to his kingdom."

I wonder if Mary could wrap her mind around the idea of a kingdom that would never end; I'm sure she struggled with it as much as we sometimes do. Unfathomable at times to comprehend, yes, and yet, it's our ultimate hope; it's the hope we look forward to and expect.

I wonder what kind of hope Jesus gave Mary as he grew up. As she encountered person after person who offered unsolicited confirmation that he was the Messiah (the shepherds and wisemen; Simeon and Anna), did it bolster her hope? Did it excite her? Did it fill her with wonder? She seems to have been the type of woman who did more thinking than reacting. We're told that after giving birth to Jesus in a stable filled with hay and animals, with shepherds suddenly showing up with their sheep, she "treasured up all these things and pondered them in her heart" (Luke 2:19 NIV).

I wonder if, as she watched Jesus grow and saw his ministry in action, she thought back to those moments with the angel or remembered Simeon's prayer after he saw Jesus: "For my eyes have seen your salvation, which you have prepared in the sight of all people" (Luke 2:30–31 NIV). Maybe these words were in the back of her mind when she calmly but firmly prompted Jesus to perform the first of his miracles recorded in the Bible, when he turned water into wine (John 2:1–11). How often did she reflect on the hope that Jesus brought, not just to her but to all people?

Mary had the privilege to witness the most incredible miracle ever known to man besides the act of creation — the virgin birth of Jesus. Though we will never see such an act like that in our own lives, miracles do still occur for each of us.

I still remember the day God healed my voice. I was a senior in high school and was singing the lead role for our spring musical when I developed a nodule (a type of blister) on one vocal cord, which made my voice raspy. The doctor put me on voice rest for three weeks to heal. Toward the end of the three weeks, I tried to hum a few notes but got the same raspy results. That Sunday morning, my mother and I went down to the front of our church during a time of prayer and prayed that God would heal my voice. That afternoon, sitting in my room reading a passage of Scripture, I felt like God was telling me to sit up and start singing. So I did, and every note came out strong and clear, even the high ones! The next morning I excitedly ran to tell my choral director that God had healed my voice. I had no more problems after that.

Maybe you have experienced healing in your life, or unexplained things that can't be chalked up to coincidence. I think God uses signs of the supernatural to give us hope in the eternal; it's his way of saying, "If you think this is great, just wait until heaven!"

Mary Magdalene also was a witness to a miracle of world-changing proportions. She was one of Jesus' followers throughout his ministry and is mentioned in several lists of women who served with his disciples. Like the Twelve, it must have been so hard for Mary and the other women who followed Jesus to understand all that happened during Jesus' arrest, trial, and crucifixion.

I wonder how Mary felt, walking with the other women to the tomb that day. Had her hope left completely? Did she feel abandoned? The disciples had all scattered, though a few, like Peter and John, were nearby. But they weren't looking too dependable at that moment. Where was her hope now? What did she have to look forward to? She had put her hope in Jesus, and they had nailed him to a cross. Had she been wrong? Had he been wrong?

But then she saw it — a gaping hole in the entrance of Jesus' tomb instead of the rock that should have been covering it. Without going in, she went to find Peter and John. "They have taken the Lord out of the tomb, and we don't know where they have put him!" she told them frantically (John 20:2 NIV).

None of them — the women or the disciples — understood from the Scriptures yet that Jesus had to rise from the dead. After Peter and John saw the strips of burial cloth folded neatly in a corner of the tomb, they had an interesting reaction. They went home (John 20:10). But Mary stayed.

Crying outside the tomb, no doubt mourning the loss not just of Jesus' life but now of his body, Mary Magdalene looked into the tomb. She suddenly saw two angels sitting where Jesus' body had been.

"Why are you crying?" they asked (verse 14).

"They have taken my Lord away," she said, "and I don't know where they have put him" (verse 14).

Here is a moment between hopelessness and hope, a moment between no potential and incredible potential, a moment when all seemed lost just before all was found again. As Mary said these words, she turned around.

And there he was: Jesus, standing right in front of her, though at first she didn't realize it. Only when he said her name (verse 16) did she recognize her Master. She saw her Messiah. She now understood the miracle that was being planned all along.

She now understood hope.

And here is what we must understand. No matter our circumstances, the challenges of this jerking roller coaster we often find ourselves riding as military wives, no matter how lost we feel, we can always turn around and see Jesus. He is with us, he is in front of us, and he is behind us. He loves us.

He is our hope, and it is a hope that doesn't go away, a hope that never subsides, a hope that has a 100 percent guarantee. And we know it has a guarantee because he said so, his Word says so, and the miracles we see that happen today stand as testimonies to the incredible miracles that happened so long ago when God sent his Son to die for our sins and be resurrected, ensuring us a new life with him and a celebration of all the grace and love he gives.

There is not a series of steps that will make any of us God Strong. There isn't a special formula or a certain spiritual regimen you can follow that will guarantee you a conflict-free, happy Christian life. Discipline can take you only so far. What makes us God Strong is when we make ourselves more available, brokenness and all, to God's guidance and his direction. When we push back our fears and step forward in the knowledge of his grace, when we get knocked down and get back up to try again with God's help — that's being God Strong.

Being a military wife is not about how strong you are. No amount of strength in the world will prepare you for some of the things you may experience. No amount of faith can fix those things, either, sometimes. Having faith in God does not mean you will have a perfect life. But when we put our trust in God, when we take him at his Word and see him as our hope, we have joy. And peace. And grace. And we have love no matter what the storms of life may throw at us.

And when we remember all of that, we can be God Strong.

Strength Builders

"So if you're serious about living this new resurrection life with Christ, *act* like it. Pursue the things over which Christ presides. Don't shuffle along, eyes to the ground, absorbed with the things right in front of you. Look up, and be alert to what is going on around Christ—that's where the action is. See things from *his* perspective" (Colossians 3:1–2).

"Each one of these people of faith died not yet having in hand what was promised, but still believing. How did they do it? They saw it way off in the distance, waved their greeting, and accepted the fact that they were transients in this world" (Hebrews 11:13).

"Keep your eyes on *Jesus*, who both began and finished this race we're in. Study how he did it. Because he never lost sight of where he was headed—that exhilarating finish in and with God—he could put up with anything along the way: cross, shame, whatever. And now he's *there*, in the place of honor, right alongside God. When you find yourselves flagging in your faith, go over that story again, item by item, that long litany of hostility he plowed through. *That* will shoot adrenaline into your souls!" (Hebrews 12:2–3).

"God's kingdom isn't a matter of what you put in your stomach, for goodness' sake. It's what God does with your life as he sets it right, puts it together, and completes it with joy. Your task is to single-mindedly serve Christ" (Romans 14:17).

STRENGTH TRAINERS

1. How is your hope found in Christ? What does he offer you that other things don't?

2. What is hope, anyway? On a scale of 1 to 10, how hopeful are you? Why?

3. How does the hope we have in Jesus compare with any of the other truths that we've discussed in this book?

4. Out of the women in the Bible discussed in this chapter, is there one whose story resonates with you most? Who is it, and why?

EPILOGUE
GOT HOPE?

If you have made it to the end of this book and, while reading it, have found yourself unsure of whether you have a personal relationship with Jesus Christ, let me encourage you to change that today!

When we commit our lives to Christ, there is nothing else like it! You may have thought experiencing homecoming and welcoming your husband home was a rush, but when you "come home" after accepting Christ as your Savior and Lord, it's incredible!

We can find the story of God's love traced throughout the Bible, and it is truly a story of good news; it tells us that because of Jesus Christ's great love for us, and what he did for us by dying on a cross and conquering death, we can be forgiven and live forever in heaven with him.

But this gift of forgiveness can't just be handed out. Each person must accept the gift individually. God wants a response from you and you alone. You can't get to heaven by being a good person or by belonging to a good family. God's gift of forgiveness is just that—a gift—but you must ask for it.

These Bible verses explain why we need forgiveness and how we go about receiving it:

God loves you completely. "For God so loved the world that he gave his one and only Son, that whoever believes in him shall not perish but have eternal life" (John 3:16 NIV).

God loves you and wants to fill your life to the fullest. He wants to give you a life that will last forever, even after your physical death.

All of us are sinners. "For all have sinned and fall short of the glory of God" (Romans 3:23 NIV). None of us have perfect lives. All of us have done things that are wrong. The Bible recognizes this when it says that all of us have sinned. As a result, we all feel separated from God, who is good and holy.

Sin comes with a price. "For the wages of sin is death, but the gift of God is eternal life in Christ Jesus our Lord" (Romans 6:23 NIV). As sinners, we must pay a penalty, just as criminals must pay for their crimes. If sin continues to control your life, spiritual death is the price that will be required of you. You will die physically, but you will also be separated from God for eternity. The Bible teaches that those who choose to stay separated from God will spend the rest of eternity in hell.

But Christ has paid our price. "But God demonstrates his own love for us in this: While we were still sinners, Christ died for us" (Romans 5:8 NIV). The Bible tells us that Jesus Christ, God's only sinless Son, paid the price for our sins. He loves you enough to die for you. You can do everything possible to have a good life or to live as a good person, but it doesn't matter; Jesus died for your sins out of love despite the things you've done.

God's free gift to you. "For it is by grace you have been saved, through faith — and this not from yourselves, it is the gift of God—not by works, so that no one can boast" (Ephesians 2:8–9 NIV). Grace is something you can never offer yourself; it's forgiveness and favor that only God can offer you. His gift to you is free; it doesn't cost anything. All he asks is that you receive it by believing in your heart that Jesus Christ died for you.

Christ is waiting. "Here I am! I stand at the door and knock. If anyone hears my voice and opens the door, I will come in and eat with him, and he with me" (Revelation 3:20 NIV). Jesus Christ wants to know you personally. He wants a close relationship with you. Invite him into your life; he's waiting, ready for you to receive him into your heart and start a new relationship with him today.

Acknowledgments

I need to thank the many people who helped make this book possible. First, I am so grateful to the wonderful team at Zondervan — particularly, editor extraordinaire Angela Scheff and marketing guru Tom Dean. Thank you for seeing the need for and the importance of this book and for your desire to bless and encourage military spouses. Thanks also to my awesome agent, Beth Jusino, and the great staff at Alive Communications.

I also want to say thanks to my writer and author friend Jennifer Schuchmann: I'm grateful for the prayers you've prayed for me and the laughter we've shared over the phone and in person as we both have journeyed together through this writing life. You may not be a military wife, but you have supported this one, which has meant so much to me.

Thank you to the ladies who belonged to that very first Wives of Faith group — Jen, Kate, Emily, Chris, and Beckie, to name just a few. You were such a blessing to me as I was going through my own deployment. Also, many ladies have jumped in over the last couple of years to share their special talents and gifts with the same vision of encouraging military wives — Anna, Allison, Shauna, Kristie, Carol, Pattie, Stephanie, and Leanne. Thank you for helping and for serving on top of everything else you do for your families and others.

I am grateful to Cliff, my husband, my best friend, and the world's greatest dad to our son. You are my steady rock through life's hectic storms and writing deadlines. I love you, and I am so proud of your service to our country. Caleb, I love it when you tell me I'm your favorite mom. You are most definitely my favorite son.

Finally, let me thank all of the military wives I've come into contact with over the last few years, for the stories you've shared with me, the good and the bad, the hope and the heartache. I believe that all of us have something we can learn from each other and that God can use us all to encourage one another.

Heavenly Father, thank you for this journey you've put me on. May the words inside this book encourage and inspire others always to seek your face before anything else. May we all one day know as your children what it means to be God Strong.

NOTES

1. Of course, there are also women out there who take the opposite approach. They willingly let others do everything for them. They convince themselves, or let others convince them, that they are helpless to do anything. If this describes you, then know that God provides strength for you too. He will equip you with what you need in order to accomplish his will for your life and your family members' lives.

2. C. S. Lewis, *Mere Christianity* (1952, 1980; New York: HarperCollins, 2001), 141.

3. Debbie Macomber, *Knit Together: Discover God's Pattern for Your Life* (New York: FaithWords/Hachette, 2007), 38–39.

4. John Drescher, "If I Were Starting My Life Again," *Daily Guideposts*, March 1979. See http://www.dailyguideposts .com/newsletter/july06/starting.asp.

5. John Ortberg, *If You Want to Walk on Water, You've Got to Get out of the Boat* (Grand Rapids: Zondervan, 2001), 118.

6. Madeleine L'Engle, *Walking on Water* (Colorado Springs, CO: WaterBrook, 2006), 82–83.

7. See http://www.sabda.org/netbible6/illustration/2532.

8. Susie Larson, *Alone in Marriage* (Chicago: Moody, 2007), 70.

9. Commentary sidebar "The Book of Ruth" in the *NIV Study Bible* (Grand Rapids: Zondervan, 1995), 362.

10. "Fast Facts: Divorce in the Military," *Navy Times*, January 12, 2009, 6.

11. Elizabeth Fletcher, "Houses and Tents," *Archaeology of the Bible*, http://www.bible-archaeology.info/housing.htm.

12. United States Department of Labor Bureau of Labor Statistics, "Number of Jobs Held, Labor Market Activity, and Earnings Growth among the Youngest Baby Boomers: Results from a Longitudinal Survey Summary," June 27, 2008, http://www.bls.gov/news.release/nlsoy.nr0.htm.

13. John Locke's "Essay Concerning Human Understanding" (1689).

14. William Marshall, *Eternity Shut in a Span*, http://www.sabda.org/netbible6/illustration/8780.

15. Study notes for John 4:10, *The NIV Study Bible*, Tenth Anniversary Study Edition (Grand Rapids: Zondervan, 1995).

CONNECTING

CONTACT SARA

I love hearing from other military wives about their joys, trials, and whatever God has laid on their hearts to share. If something you've read has touched you, if you've asked Jesus into your life and want to let me know, or if you'd just like to contact me to say hello, please do! You can do so in several different ways:

Email me at sara@sarahorn.com.

Write to me at Sara Horn, 5016 Spedale Ct., #354, Spring Hill, TN 37174.

Add me as a friend on Facebook (facebook.com/ sarahorn) and/or follow me on Twitter (@sarahorn).

Looking forward to hearing from you!

SPEAKING OPPORTUNITIES

I love to speak to military spouses even more than I love writing to them. Are you reading *God Strong* with a group of other wives? Invite me to call in through Skype for a fun "get to know the author" session! I would love to talk with your group more on what it means to be God Strong.

Do you have a spouse brunch or FRG meeting coming up? Would you like me to speak at your next spouse club meeting or military association conference? Send your query to requests@sarahorn.com.

Topics I speak on include:

- Keeping Strong Marriages
- Dealing with Deployment
- Staying Positive in a Negative World
- Ways to Help Your Kids during Deployment
- Facing Your Fears

BIBLE STUDY NOTES

For online study guides you can use as an individual or for your small group, visit www.godstrongbook.com

RESOURCES

There are many wonderful resources out there to benefit the military spouse. Please visit my website at www.sarahorn .com for the latest updated list.

CREATE CONNECTION

As we've discussed in *God Strong*, we military wives often try to do things on our own, not looking for help from God or anyone else. We convince ourselves we're okay, but we don't realize the joy, fun, laughter, and support we're missing when we don't have others to share this journey of military life together.

I've often told others that some of the best times I've experienced have been with other military wives at a Wives of Faith meeting or get-together. There is something so encouraging and positive about being with other women who share your challenges but also share your faith. They not only know the importance of praying for you but also know *how* to pray for you. It's an incredible difference I wish every military wife could experience.

If you find yourself wishing you had this kind of support system, then let me suggest that you start with this book. Invite a group of military wives—maybe they're in your church, maybe they are part of your spouse club or in your neighborhood—to read and discuss the chapters together. Then keep meeting! Whether your group meets through your church or an organization like Wives of Faith, all it takes is a willingness to make a difference not only in your own life but also in the lives of others.

Want more information? Visit www.wivesoffaith.org to learn more about creating a local WoF chapter or starting a local support group for military wives in your community.

Share Your Thoughts

With the Author: Your comments will be forwarded to the author when you send them to *zauthor@zondervan.com*.

With Zondervan: Submit your review of this book by writing to *zreview@zondervan.com*.

Free Online Resources at
www.zondervan.com

Zondervan AuthorTracker: Be notified whenever your favorite authors publish new books, go on tour, or post an update about what's happening in their lives at www.zondervan.com/authortracker.

Daily Bible Verses and Devotions: Enrich your life with daily Bible verses or devotions that help you start every morning focused on God. Visit www.zondervan.com/newsletters.

Free Email Publications: Sign up for newsletters on Christian living, academic resources, church ministry, fiction, children's resources, and more. Visit www.zondervan.com/newsletters.

Zondervan Bible Search: Find and compare Bible passages in a variety of translations at www.zondervanbiblesearch.com.

Other Benefits: Register yourself to receive online benefits like coupons and special offers, or to participate in research.

ZONDERVAN®

ZONDERVAN.com/
AUTHORTRACKER
follow your favorite authors